ELEC

GRAVITICS

SYSTEMS

Volume I

Thomas Valone, PhD

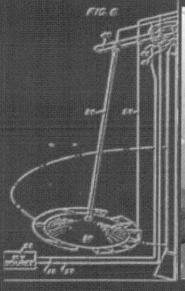

ELECTROGRAVITICS SYSTEMS

Volume I

REPORTS ON A NEW PROPULSION METHODOLOGY

Edited by

Thomas Valone, Ph.D., P.E.

Foreword by *Elizabeth Rauscher, Ph.D.*

Integrity Research Institute

nonprofit 501(c)3 organization

for T. Townsend Brown

gratitude to T. Townsend Brown, Electric Spacecraft Journal, Paul
LaViolette, Aviation Studies, Steve Hall, Charles Yost, Larry
Deavenport, Elizabeth Rauscher, Banesh Hoffman, Leslie Kulba,
Peter Hunt, Alexander Frolov for their contributions.

Reprinted by permission from original publisher:
INTEGRITY RESEARCH INSTITUTE
www.Integrity-Research.org

Electrogravitics Systems Volume I: Reports on a New Propulsion
Methodology

Edited by Thomas F. Valone, PhD

First Edition, April, 1994
Sixth Edition, July, 2008
Seventh Edition, July 2023

Rights further assigned to publisher:

JT Pro Investments, LLC
5020 Sunnyside Avenue, Suite 216, Beltsville MD 20705

Library of Congress Cataloging-in-Publication Data
Valone, Thomas
Electrogravitics Systems: reports on a new propulsion methodology
ISBN 9798852929204

1.   Aeronautics.   2. Antigravity – Research – United States.
3. Electrostatics – Research – United States.
I. Title
TL507.E43 1995
629.1 dc20

CONTENTS

FOREWORD

by Elizabeth Rauscher, Ph.D.
Professor of Nuclear and Astrophysics, University of Nevada

Electromagnetism is bipolar, i.e. it attracts and repels. We can shield X-rays, gamma rays, radio waves, etc., but what about gravity? Gravity appears to have only one polarity – attraction! We have balloons, planes, and rockets that <u>overcome</u> gravity but can we build a shield against gravity? Roger Babson, a good friend of Thomas Edison, established the Gravity Research Foundation in 1948 at Edison's suggestion. So what would anti-gravity "look like"? Let us explore these issues:

Standard physical models include *four* fundamental forces in Nature. They are the nuclear force, the electromagnetic force, the weak, nuclear decay force, and gravitational force. The nuclear force and the gravitational force have the similar property of being attractive only. What of anti-matter – does it rise in a gravitational field? Such an experiment was attempted at the Stanford Linear Accelerator Center, Stanford, CA without confirmed results.

In 1971, I published a book and several papers on a ten dimensional geometric model of quantum gravity in which I treated the four major force fields on an "equal footing" in such a manner as to consider them as *bi* or dual polar, having both attraction and repulsion.

T. Townsend Brown, who I met in 1981, led me to replicate his research on some properties of electrostatics, capacitance and anomalous current flows on unique materials. Unlike the current view, electrostatic phenomena are very complex. How does this work relate to the ideas of UFO propulsion (an early interest of T.T. Brown)? Certainly he has presented the scientific community with many questions we need to investigate.

I have also theoretically examined a five and eight dimensional geometry which includes the Kaluza Klein geometry which is an abstract formalism relating electromagnetism to the gravitational field. This model interested Albert Einstein in the 1930's. There is a long path between theoretical concepts, romantic wishes and preliminary experiments to detailed experimental verification and actual designed technology.

4

Let us re-examine Brown's works and rethink some of the issues which he has suggested to us. Science is an ongoing process, not a fixed set of facts, ever changing and developing.

Prof. Elizabeth A. Rauscher, Ph.D.

PREFACE to the 5ᵗʰ Edition

This edition marks the 10ᵗʰ anniversary of the delivery of the first operational B-2 stealth bomber by Northrop Grumman and the publication of this book. Many events have transpired in the past decade to vindicate the electrogravitics discovery by T. T. Brown that it may be helpful to review some of them to bring the reader up to date. Keep in mind that ion ("lifter") flow and air drag reduction are secondary and sometimes unrelated effects if the voltage is low.

- This year, for the first time, I talked with a Maryland eyewitness to a late night flight of the B-2 with two chase planes. He told me that he could clearly see the bright violet glow around the fighter, which verifies the presence of a high voltage corona in the million-volt range. In my opinion, it would be a good promotional move for Northrop to release a nighttime photograph "with flame jet voltage on" to revive the public interest in the aging aircraft.

- Several testimonials have appeared from military personnel that corroborate the presence of electrogravitics on the B-2 stealth bomber, such as from retired AF Col. Donald Ware.

- The use of high voltage on the leading edge of the wing now has wider industrial support for its dramatic aerodynamic ability to reduce air turbulence and drag. Festo AG sponsored its first subsonic separation flow control experiments in 1999 with on and off photos to prove its ability to restore laminar flow.[1]

- Plasma actuators (dielectric electrodes on the wings) became an active area of research by the AFRL in 2003 to reduce drag, replacing slats, flaps and slots, with an ability to reattach separated flow at high angles of attack.[2]

- In 2001, a surprising capacitor NASA patent #6,317,310 "for creating a thrust force" issued without any reference to T. T. Brown's prior art patents.

- An international PCT patent WO 00/58623, issued in 2000, uses an electrified plurality of high dielectric cells to produce thrust.

- Dr. T. Musha from Honda published experimental results in 2004 that agree well with the theory. Musha says the force generated by the external electric field is due to a new gravitational field generated at the micro level

---

[1] 17 kV experiments – http://www.zukunftswerkstatt-elektrofluidsysteme.de/index2.html

[2] http://www.gerc.eng.ufl.edu/Research%20Institute/afosr_workshop.htm

induced by strong coupling between electromagnetism and gravitation. See complete article in *Electrogravitics II.*

- Mark McCandlish released in 2001 a detailed drawing of a circular craft on display by Col. T. Horning at Norton AFB in 1988 that uses a series of pulsed HV capacitors with high dielectrics for upward thrust.[3]

Thomas Valone, Ph.D.
April, 2004

---

[3] McCandlish, Mark in *Disclosure* by S. Greer, Crossing Point, Crozet, VA, 2001, p. 497-510

PREFACE to the 1ˢᵗ Edition

"Newton attempted to explain the force of gravity on two hypotheses: the existence of a medium, or ether, and action at a distance. The first hypothesis he rejected as being physically absurd, the second as contrary to reason. Newton had, therefore, no theory of gravity. However, his long and sustained effort to understand gravity was not without at least one serious consequence. For involvement in the ether theory obscured from Newton the universal character of the inverse-square relation, and delayed for twenty years his final formulation of the law of gravity."[4]

Many people have had the opportunity to meet and learn from T. Townsend Brown before he passed away about a decade ago. I was fortunate to correspond with him after I returned from the Gravity Field Energy Conference in Germany, 1980, where his name was mentioned a lot. He was a friendly but quiet person who learned some of his magic from Dr. Paul Alfred Biefeld, a physicist at the California Institute for Advanced Studies. "In 1923, Biefeld discovered that a heavily charged electrical condenser moved toward its positive pole when suspended in a gravitational field. He assigned Brown to study the effect as a research project."[5]

The *Electric Spacecraft Journal* also notes that Brown's effect may have an earlier precedent as well, citing an article by Nipher.[6] Whomever deserves credit, the question today is the credibility of T. T. Brown and whether his effect is significant for propulsion.

It can be argued that if the two main reports of this anthology are historically valid, Brown may have been debriefed after his release from military consultation service. The interesting fact

---

[4] Evans, *American Journal of Physics*, 26, 619, 1958

[5] Pawlicki, *How to Build a Flying Saucer*, Prentice-Hall, 1981 (also see *Ether-Technology: A Rational Approach to Gravity-Control*, Rho Sigma, 1977, p.33)

[6] Nipher, *Electrical Experimenter*, March, 1918, p.743

about the first report is that under the black streak, prominently seen across the original title page, the word "CONFIDENTIAL" actually was written. Dr. Paul LaViolette notes that the *Electrogravitics Systems* report may be obtained from the Wright-Patterson AFB technical library, even though it is not actually listed on their library computer. He found that it is not available from any other library in the U.S. Paul deserves our gratitude for retrieving the first report.

To authenticate the discovery of these two reports, I have included a copy of the 1956 *Gravitics Situation* "Order Form," as well as copies of the original title pages for *Electrogravitics Systems*.

I feel that it is important to mention that even though Talley has, in 1991, attempted a replication of Brown's work, up to 19 kV (and 33 kV with anomalous breakdown effects) for Edwards AFB,[7] we see in these uncovered reports, mention of the "magic number" of 50,000, with a target wattage of 50,000 kW and a dielectric K value of 50,000. Brown is also quoted as recommending heating of the cathode.

Many people have tried low voltage replication (e.g. Dr. Harold Puthoff...17 kV) but these reports indicate that higher voltage is better, up to a maximum effect.

Cravens, also a recent military consultant, gives Brown a high rating for practicality and notes that older high voltage supplies most likely had time-varying voltage regulation signals superimposed upon the DC electrostatic voltage.[8] This fact, along with the similar Hutchison effect signal, may point the way toward an overlooked detail in the race to replicate T.T. Brown.[9]

---

[7] Talley, "Twenty First Century Propulsion Concept" Phillips Lab, AFSC, Propulsion Directorate, Edwards AFB CA, PL-TR-91-3009, May, 1991

[8] Cravens, "Electric Propulsion Study" Astronautics Lab, AFSC, Edwards AFB CA, AL-TR-89-040, Aug., 1990

[9] Hathaway, "The Hutchison Effect – A Lift and Disruption System" New Energy Technology, Planetary Association for Clean Energy,

As this book goes to press, *Science* magazine notes Puthoff, Haisch and Rueda presenting a new theory of inertia which they say raises a "provocative notion: that inertia, once understood, might be controlled."[10] This underscores our return to T. T. Brown and his research because of its simplicity.

I have included an extra article by Dr. Banesh Hoffman, the biographer of Einstein, because he also theorized about negative mass, the concept which Gravity Rand Ltd. believes holds a key to understanding the Biefeld-Brown effect.

What can be said about Dr. LaViolette's well-researched sleuth about the B-2 aircraft? It is a provocative thesis which presents a plausible modern application of Brown's research. As more facts are uncovered, we will consider future additions to the Electrogravitics series.[11]

Thomas Valone, 1994
Physicist and Prof. Engineer

Hull, Quebec, 1988, p. 77

[10] Matthews, "Inertia: Does Empty Space Put Up the Resistance?" *Science,* Vol. 263, Feb., 1994, p. 612

[11] *Electrogravitics II* was published in 2004 for the 10th anniversary of the B-2 – Ed. note

AVIATION STUDIES (INTERNATIONAL) LIMITED

Aviation House, 66 Sloane St. London, S.W.1 Tel. SLO. 0657/8. Cables AVIANCE LONDON

THE GRAVITICS SITUATION

A new report of interest both to management and to engineers will be available in Mid-December. The section for engineers is in three parts; first is an assault on the quantum mechanical approach to the existence of negative mass: this is supported by Bozer's paper, who in turn looks to Schrodinger's time independent equation with the center of mass motion removed. A second approach is electrogravitics, which is Townsend Brown's work, and the report contains a complete specification of Brown's gravitator device and a survey of this branch of activity. Third is an outline of possible ways of finding the link between gravitational fields and nuclear energy which draws on Beaumont's complex spin, Deser, Arnowitt and Bondi. This section is supported by Deser and Arnowitt's proposition, as they expressed it. This part is perhaps the most important of all.

For management there is a section dealing with the impact of various approaches on company policy; this includes a rough estimation of the value of current work. This section also includes a glossary of terms in an attempt to prevent the dictionary running away with the science, together with Gravity Rand observations. (Fee $30: £10)

To: Gravity Rand Ltd,
Aviation House, 66 Sloane Street,
London S.W.1, England

Please send us your report. "THE GRAVITICS SITUATION
● We enclose $ (£)..............................(Payment should be made out to:
AVIATION STUDIES (INTERNATIONAL) LIMITED).
● Invoice us later

Name....................."THE GRAVITICS SITUATION

Address: (to be used for mailing)....................

11

ELECTROGRAVITICS SYSTEMS

An examination of electrostatic motion,
dynamic counterbary and barycentric control.

AVIATION STUDIES (INTERNATIONAL) LTD.

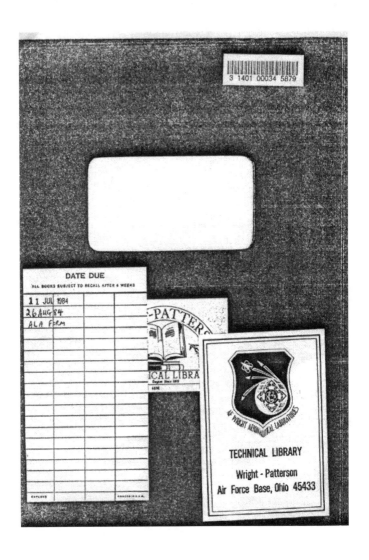
13

ELECTROGRAVITICS SYSTEMS

An examination of electrostatic motion, dynamic counterbary and barycentric control.

AVIATION STUDIES (INTERNATIONAL) LTD.

Prepared by:
Gravity Research Group
Special Weapons Study Unit
Aviation Studies (International) Limited, London.
29-31 Cheval Place, Knightsbridge
London, S,W,7 England

Report GRG-013/56 February 1956

CONTENTS

Introductory Notes

Discussion

Conclusions

APPENDIX

14

ELECTROGRAVITICS SYSTEMS

An examination of electrostatic motion,
Dynamic counterbary and barycentric control

It has been accepted as axiomatic that the way to offset the effects of gravity is to use a lifting surface and considerable molecular energy to produce a continuously applied force that, for a limited period of time, can remain greater than the effects of gravitational attraction. The original invention of the glider, and evolution of the briefly self-sustaining glider, at the turn of the century led to progressive advances in power and knowledge. This has been directed to refining the classic Wright Brothers' approach. Aircraft design is still fundamentally as the Wrights adumbrated it, with wings, body, tails, moving or flapping controls, landing gear and so forth. The Wright biplane was a powered glider, and all subsequent aircraft, including the supersonic jets of the nineteen-fifties are also powered gliders. Only one fundamentally different flying principle has so far been adopted with varying degrees of success. It is the rotating wing aircraft that has led to the jet lifters and vertical pushers, coleopters, ducted fans and lift induction turbine propulsion systems.

But during these decades there was always the possibility of making efforts to discover the nature of gravity from cosmic or quantum theory, investigation and observation, with a view to discerning the physical properties of aviations' enemy.

It has seemed to Aviation Studies that for some time insufficient attention has been directed to this kind of

15

research. If it were successful such developments would change the concept of sustentation, and confer upon a vehicle qualities that would now be regarded as the ultimate in aviation.

This report summarizes in simple form the work that has been done and is being done in the new field of electrogravitics. It also outlines the various possible lines of research into the nature and constituent matter of gravity, and how it has changed from Newton to Einstein to the modern Hlavaty concept of gravity as an electromagnetic force that may be controlled like a light wave.

The report also contains an outline of opinions on the feasibility of different electrogravitics systems and there is reference to some of the barycentric control and electrostatic rigs in operation.

Also included is a list of references to electrogravitics in successive Aviation Reports since a drive was started by Aviation Studies (International) Limited to suggest to aviation business eighteen months ago that the rewards of success are too far-reaching to be overlooked, especially in view of the hopeful judgement of the most authoritative voices in microphysics. Also listed are some relevant patents on electrostatics and electrostatic generators in the United States, United Kingdom and France.

Gravity Research Group

DISCUSSION

Electrogravitics might be described as a synthesis of electrostatic energy use for propulsion - either vertical propulsion or horizontal or both - and gravitics, or dynamic conterbary, in which energy is also used to set up a local gravitational force independent of the earth's.

Electrostatic energy for propulsion has been predicted as a possible means of propulsion in space when the thrust from a neutron motor or ion motor would be sufficient in a dragless environment to produce astronomical velocities. But the ion motor is not strictly a part of the science of electrogravitics, since barycentric control in an electrogravitics system is envisaged for a vehicle operating within the earth's environment and it is not seen initially for space application. Probably large scales space operations would have to await the full development of electrogravitics to enable large pieces of equipment to be moved out of the region of the earth's strongest gravity effects. So, though electrostatic motors were thought of in 1925, electrogravitics had its birth after the War, when Townsend Brown sought to improve on the various proposals that then existed for electrostatic motors sufficiently to produce some visible manifestation of sustained motion. Whereas earlier electrostatic test were essentially pure research. Brown's rigs were aimed from the outset at producing a flying article. As a private venture he produced evidence of motion using condensers in a couple of saucers suspended by arms rotating round a central tower with input running down the arms. The massive-k situation was summarized subsequently in a report, Project Winterhaven, in 1952. Using the data some conclusions were arrived at that might be expected from ten or more years of intensive development -similar to that, for instance, applied to the turbine engine. Using a number of assumptions as to the nature of gravity, the report postulated a saucer as the basis of a possible interceptor with Mach 3 capability. Creation of a local gravitational system would confer upon the fighter the sharp-edged changes of direction typical of motion in space.

The essence of electrogravitics thrust is the use of a very strong positive charge on one side of the vehicle and a negative on the other. The core of the motor is a condenser and the ability of the condenser to hold its charge (the K-number) is the yardstick of performance. With air as 1, current dielectrical materials can yield 6 and use of barium aluminate can raise this considerable, barium titanium oxide (a baked ceramic) can offer 6,000 and there is promise of 30,000, which would be sufficient for supersonic speed.

The original Brown rig produced 30 fps on a voltage of around 50,000 and a small amount of current in the milliamp range. There was no detailed explanation of gravity in Project Winterhaven, but it was assumed that particle dualism in the subatomic structure of gravity would coincide in its effect with the issuing stream of electrons from the electrostatic energy source to produce counterbary. The Brown work probably remains a realistic approach to the practical realization of electrostatic propulsion and sustentation. Whatever may be discovered by the Gravity Research Foundation of New Boston a complete understanding and synthetic reproduction of gravity is not essential for limited success. The electrogravitics saucer can perform the function of a classic lifting surface - it produces a pushing effect on the under surface and a suction effect on the upper, but, unlike the airfoil, it does not require a flow of air to produce the effect.

First attempts at electogravitics are unlikely to produce counterbary, but may lead to development of an electrostatic VTOL vehicle. Even in its developed form this might be an advance on the molecular heat engine in its capabilities. But hopes in the new science depend on an understanding of the close identity of electrostatic motivating forces with the source and matter of gravity. It is fortuitous that lift can be produced in the traditional fashion and if an understanding of gravity remains beyond full practical control, electrostatic lift might be an adjunct of some significance to modern thrust producers. Research into electrostatics could prove beneficial to turbine development, and heat engines in general, in view of the usable electron potential round the periphery of any flame. Material for electrogravitics and especially the development of commercial quantities of high-k material is another dividend to be obtained from electrostatic research even if it produces no counterbary. This is a line of development that Aviation Studies' Gravity Research Group is following.

One of the interesting aspects of electrogravitics is that a breakthrough in almost any part of the broad front of general research on the intranuclear processes may be translated into a meaningful advance toward the feasibility of electrogravitics systems. This demands constant monitoring in the most likely areas of the physics of high energy sub-nuclear particles. It is difficult to be overoptimistic about the prospects of gaining so complete a grasp of gravity while the world's physicists are still engaged in a study of fundamental particles -that is to say those that cannot be broken down any more. Fundamental particles are still being discovered - the most recent was the Segre-Chamberlain-Wiegand attachment to the bevatron, which was used to isolate the missing anti-proton, which must - or should be presumed to - exist according to Dirac's theory of the electron. Much of the accepted mathematics of particles would be wrong if the anti-proton was proved to be non-existent. Earlier Eddington has listed the fundamental particles as:

e. The charge of an electron.

m. The mass of an electron.

M. The mass of proton.

h. Planck's constant

c. The velocity of light.

G. The constant of gravitation, and

Λ.. The cosmical constant.

It is generally held that no one of these can be inferred from the others. But electrons may will disappear from among the fundamental particles, though, as Russell says, it is likely that *e* and *m* will survive. The constants are much more established than the interpretation of them and are among the most solid of achievements in modern physics.

* * * *

Gravity may be defined as a small scale departure from Euclidean space in the general theory of relativity. The gravitational constant is one of four dimensionless constants: first, the mass relation of the nucleon and electron. Second is e^2/hc, third, the Compton wavelength of the proton, and fourth is the gravitational constant, which is the ration of the electrostatic to the gravitational attraction between the electron and the proton.

One of the stumbling blocks in electrogravitics is the absence of any satisfactory theory linking these four dimensionless quantities. Of the four, moreover, gravity is decidedly the most complex, since any explanation would have to satisfy both cosmic and quantum relations more acceptably and intelligibly even than the unified field theory. A gravitational constant of around 10^{-39} has emerged from quantum research and this has been used as a tool for finding theories that could link the two relations. This work is now in full progress, and developments have to be watched for the aviation angle. Hitherto Dirac, Eddington, Jordan and others have produced differences in theory that are too wide to be accepted as consistent. It means therefore that (i) without a cosmical basis, and (ii) with an imprecise quantum basis and (iii) a vague hypothesis on the interaction, much remains still to be discovered. Indeed some say that a single interacting theory to link up the dimensionless constants is one of three major unresolved basic problems of physics. The other two main problems are the extension of quantum theory and a more detailed knowledge of the fundamental particles.

All this is some distance from Newton, who saw gravity as a force acting on a body from a distance, leading to the tendency of bodies to accelerate towards each other. He allied this assumption with Euclidean geometry, and time was assumed as uniform and acted independently of space. Bodies and particles in space normally moved uniformly in straight lines according to Newton, and to account for the way they sometimes do not do so, he used the idea of a force of gravity acting at a distance, in which particles of matter cause in others an acceleration proportional to their mass, and inversely proportional to the square of the distance between them.

But Einstein showed how the principle of least action, or the so-called cosmic laziness means that particles, on the contrary, follow the easiest path along geodesic lines and as a result they get readily absorbed into space-time. So was born non-linear physics. The classic example of non-linear physics is the experiment in bombarding a screen with two slits. When both slits are open particles going through are not the sum of the two individually but follows a non-linear equation. This leads on to wave-particle dualism and that in turn to the Heisenberg uncertainty principle in which an increase in accuracy in measurement of one physical quantity means decreasing accuracy in measuring the other. If time is measured accurately energy calculations will be in error; the more accurate the position of a particle is established the less certain the velocity will be; and so on. This basic principle of causality of microphysics affects the study of gravity in the special and general theories of relativity. Lack of pictorial image in the quantum physics of this interrelationship is a difficulty at the outset for those whose minds remain obstinately Euclidean.

In the special theory of relativity, space-time is seen only as an undefined interval which can be defined in any way that is convenient and the Newtonian idea of persistent particles in motion to explain gravity cannot be accepted. It must be seen rather as a synthesis of forces in a four dimensional continuum, three to establish the position and one the time. The general theory of relativity that followed a decade later was a geometrical explanation of gravitation in which bodies take the geodesic path through space-time. In turn this means that instead of the idea of force acting at a distance it is assumed that space, time, radiation and particles are linked and variations in them from gravity are due rather to the nature of space.

Thus gravity of a body such as the earth, instead of pulling objects towards it as Newton postulated, is adjusting the characteristics of space and, it may be inferred, the quantum mechanics of space in the vicinity of the gravitational force. Electrogravitics aims at correcting this adjustment to put matter, so to speak, 'at rest'.

* * * *

One of the difficulties in 1954 and 1955 was to get aviation to take electrogravitics seriously. The name alone was enough to put people off. However, in the trade much progress has been made and now most major companies in the United States are interested in counterbary. Groups are being organized to study electrostatic and electromagnetic phenomena. Most of industry's leaders have made some reference to it. Douglas has now stated that it has counterbary on its work agenda by does not expect results yet awhile. Hiller has referred to new forms of flying platform, Glenn Martin say gravity control could be achieved in six years, but they add that it would entail a Manhattan District type of effort to bring it about. Sikorsky, one of the pioneers, more or less agrees with the Douglas verdict and says that gravity is tangible and formidable, but there must be a physical carrier for this immense trans-spatial force. This implies that where a physical manifestation exists, a physical device can be developed for creating a similar force moving in the opposite direction to cancel it. Clarke Electronics state they have a rig, and add that in their view the source of gravity's force will be understood sooner than some people think. General Electric is working on the use of electronic rigs designed to make adjustments to gravity - this line of attack has the advantage of using rigs already in existence for other defence work. Bell also has an experimental rig intended, as the company puts it, to cancel out gravity, and Lawrence Bell has said he is convinced that practical hardware will emerge from current programs. Grover Leoning is certain that what he referred to as an electromagnetic contra-gravity mechanism will be developed for practical use. Convair is extensively committed to the work with several rigs. Lear Inc., autopilot and electronic engineers have a division of the company working on gravity research and so also has the Sperry division of Sperry-Rand. This list embraces most of the U.S. aircraft industry. The remainder, Curtiss-Wright, Lockheed, Boeing and North American have not yet declared themselves, but all these four are known to be in various stages of study with and without rigs.

In addition, the Massachusetts Institute of Technology is working on gravity, the Gravity Research Foundation of New Boston, the Institute for Advanced Study at Princeton, the CalTech Radiation Laboratory, Princeton University and the University of North Carolina are all active in gravity. Glenn L. Martin is setting up a Research Institute of Advanced Study which has a small staff working on gravity research with the unified field theory and this group is committed to extensive programs of applied research. Many others are also known to be studying gravity, some are known also to be planning a general expansion in this field, such as in the proposed Institute for Pure Physics at the University of North Carolina.

A certain amount of work is also going on in Europe. One of the French nationalized constructors and one company outside the nationalized elements have been making preliminary studies, and a little company money has in one case actually been committed. Some work is also going on in Britain where rigs are now in existence. Most of it is private venture work, such as that being done by Ed Hull a colleague of Townsend Brown who, as much as anybody, introduced Europe to electrogravitics. Aviation Studies' Gravity Research Group is doing some work, mainly on k studies, and is sponsoring dielectric investigations.

One Swedish company and two Canadian companies have been making studies, and quite recently the Germans have woken up to the possibilities. Several of the companies have started digging out some of the early German papers on wave physics. They are almost certain to plan a gravitics program. Curiously enough the Germans during the war paid no attention to electrogravitics. This is one line of advance that they did not pioneer in any way and it was basically a U.S. creation. Townsend Brown in electrogravitics is the equivalent of Frank Whittle in gas turbines. This German overlooking of electrostatics is even more surprising when it is remembered how astonishingly advanced and prescient the Germans were in nuclear research. (The modern theory of making thermonuclear weapons without plutonium fission initiators returns to the original German idea that was dismissed, even ridiculed. The Germans never went very far with fission, indeed they doubted that this chain would ever be made to work.) The German air industry, still in the embryo stage, has included electrogravitics among the subjects it intends to examine when establishing the policy that the individual companies will adopt after the present early stage of foreign license has enabled industry to get abreast of the other countries in aircraft development.

* * * *

It is impossible to read through this summary of the widening efforts being made to understand the nature of matter of gravity without sharing the hope that many groups now have, of major theoretical breakthroughs occurring before very long. Experience in nucleonics has shown that when attempts to win knowledge on this scale are made, advances are soon seen. There are a number of elements in industry, and some managements, who see gravity as a problem for later generations. Many see nothing in it all and they may be right. But as said earlier, if Dr. Vaclav Hlavaty thinks gravity is potentially controllable that surely should be justification enough, and indeed inspiration, for physicists to apply their minds and for management to take a risk. Hlavaty is the only man who thinks he can see a way of doing the mathematics to demonstrate Einstein's unified field theory - something that Einstein himself said was beyond him. Relativity and the unified field theory go to the root of electrogravitics and the shifts in thinking, the hopes and fears, and a measure of progress is to be obtained only in the last resort from men of this stature.

Major theoretical breakthroughs to discover the sources of gravity will be made by the most advanced intellects using the most advanced research tools. Aviation's role is therefore to impress upon physicists of this calibre with the urgency of the matter and to aid them with statistical and peripheral investigations that will help to clarify the background to the central mathematical and physical puzzles. Aviation could also assist by recruiting some of these men as advisers. Convair has taken the initiative with its recently established panel of advisers on nuclear projects, which include Dr. Edward Teller of the University of California. At the same time much can be done in development of laboratory rigs, condenser research and dielectric development, which do not require anything like the same cerebral capacity to get results and make a practical contribution.

As gravity is likely to be linked with the new particles, only the highest powered particle accelerators are likely to be of use in further fundamental knowledge. The country with the biggest tools of this kind is in the best position to examine the characteristics of the particles and from those countries the greatest advances seem most likely.

Though the United States has the biggest of the bevatrons - the Berkeley bevatron is 6.2 bev - the Russians have a 10 bev accelerator in construction which, when it is completed, will be the world's largest. At Brookhaven a 25 bev instrument is in development which, in turn, will be the biggest. Other countries without comparable facilities are of course at a great disadvantage from the outset in the contest to discover the explanation of gravity. Electrogravitics, moreover, unfortunately competes with nuclear studies for its facilities. The clearest thinking brains are bound to be attracted to localities where the most extensive laboratory equipment exists. So, one way and another, results are most likely to come from the major countries with the biggest undertakings. Thus the nuclear facilities have a direct bearing on the scope for electrogravitics work.

The OEEC report in January made the following points:

The U.S. has six to eight entirely different types of reactors in operation and many more under construction. Europe has now two different types in service.

The U.S. has about 30 research reactors plus four in Britain, two in France.

The U.S. has two nuclear-powered marine engines. Europe has none, but the U.K. is building one.

Isotope separation plants for the enrichment of uranium in the U.S. are roughly 11 times larger than the European plant in Britain.

Europe's only heavy water plant (in Norway) produces somewhat less than one-twentieth of American output.

In 1955 the number of technicians employed in nuclear energy work in the U.S. was about 15,000; there are about 5,000 in Britain, 1,800 in France, and about 1,000 in the rest of Europe. But the working party says that pessimistic conclusions should not be drawn from these comparisons. European nuclear energy effort is unevenly divided at the moment, but some countries have notable achievements to their credit and important developments in prospect. The main reason for optimism is that, taken as a whole, "Europe's present nuclear effort falls very short of its industrial potential."

Though gravity research, such as there has been of it, has been unclassified, new principles and information gained from the nuclear research facilities that have a vehicle application is expected to be withheld.

The heart of the problem to understanding gravity is likely to prove to be the way in which the very high energy sub-nuclear particles convert something, whatever it is, continuously and automatically into the tremendous nuclear and electromagnetic forces. Once this key is understood, attention can later be directed to finding laboratory means of duplicating the process and reversing its force lines in some local environment and returning the energy to itself to produce counterbary. Looking beyond it seems possible that gravitation will be shown to be a part of the universal electromagnetic processes and controlled in the same way as a light wave or radio wave. This is a synthesis of the Einstein and Hlavaty concepts. Hence it follows that though in its initial form the mechanical processes for countering gravity may initially be massive to deal with the massive forces involved, eventually this could be expected to form some central power generation unit. Barycentric control in some required quantity could be passed over a distance by a form of radio wave. The prime energy source to energize the waves would of course be nuclear in its origins.

It is difficult to say which lines of detailed development being processed in the immediate future is more likely to yield significant results. Perhaps the three most promising are: first, the new attempt by the team of men led by Chamberlain working with the Berkeley bevatron to find the anti-neutron, and to identify more of the characteristics of the anti-proton and each of the string of high energy particles that have been discovered during recent operation at 6.2 bev.[*]

A second line of approach is the United States National Bureau of Standards program to pin down with greater accuracy the acceleration value of gravity. The presently accepted figure of 32.174 feet per second per second is

---

[*]The reaction is as follows: protons are accelerated to 6.2 bev, and directed at a target of copper. When the proton projectile hits a neutron in one of the copper atoms the following emerge: the two original particles (the projectile and the struck neutron) and a new pair of particles, a proton and anti-proton. The anti-proton continues briefly until it hits another proton, then both disappear and decay into mesons.

known to be not comprehensive, though it has been sufficiently accurate for the limited needs of industry hitherto. The NBS program aims at re-determining the strength of gravity to within one part of a million. The present method has been to hold a ball 16 feet up and chart the elapsed time of descent with electronic measuring equipment. The new program is based on the old, but with this exceptional degree of accuracy it is naturally immensely more difficult and is expected to take 3 years.

A third promising line is the new technique of measuring high energy particles in motion that was started by the University of California last year. This involves passing cosmic rays through a chamber containing a mixture of gas, alcohol and water vapor. This creates charged atoms, or positive ions, by knocking electrons off the gas molecules. A sudden expansion of the chamber results in a condensation of water droplets along the track which can be plotted on a photographic plate. This method makes it easier to assess the energy of particles and to distinguish one from the other. It also helps to establish the characteristics of the different types of particle. The relationship between these high energy particles; and their origin and characteristics, have a bearing on electrogravitics in general.

So much of what has to be discovered as a necessary preliminary to gravity is of no practical use by itself. There is no conceivable use, for instance, for the anti-proton, yet its discovery even at a cost of $9-million is essential to check the mathematics of the fundamental components of matter. Similarly it is necessary to check that all the nuclear ghosts that have been postulated theoretically do in fact exist. It is not, moreover, sufficient, as in the past, only to observe the particles by radiation counters. In each instance a mechanical maze has to be devised and attached to a particle accelerator to trap only the particle concerned. Each discovery becomes a wedge for a deeper probe of the nucleus. Many of the particles of very high energy have only a fleeting existence and collisions that give rise to them from bevatron bombardment is a necessary prerequisite to an understanding of gravity. There are no shortcuts to this process.

Most of the major programs for extending human knowledge on gravity are being conducted with instruments already in use for nuclear research and to this extent the cost of work exclusively on gravitational examinations is still not of major proportions. This has made it difficult for aviation to gauge the extent of the work in progress on gravity research.

CONCLUSIONS

1. No attempts to control the magnitude or direction of the earth's gravitational force have yet been successful. But if the explanation of gravity is to be found in the as yet undetermined characteristics of the very high energy particles it is becoming increasingly possible with the bevatron to work with the constituent matter of gravity. It is therefore reasonable to expect that the new bevatron may, before long, be used to demonstrate limited gravitational control.

2. An understanding and identification of these particles is on the frontiers of human knowledge, and a full assessment of them is one of the major unresolved puzzles of the nucleus. An associated problem is to discover a theory to account for the cosmic and quantum relations of gravity, and a theory to link the gravitational constant with the other three

demensionless constants.

3. Though the obstacles to an adequate grasp of microphysics still seem formidable, the transportation rewards that could follow from electrogravitics are as high as can be envisaged. In a weightless environment, movement with sharp-edged changes of direction could offer unique manoeuvrability.

4. Determination of the environment of the anti-proton, discovery of the anti-neutron and closer examination of the other high energy particles are preliminaries to the hypothesis that gravity is one aspect of electromagnetism that may eventually be controlled like a wave. When the structure of the nucleus becomes clearer, the influence of the gravitational force upon the nucleus and the nature of its behavior in space will be more readily understood. This is a great advance on the Newtonian concept of gravity acting at a distance.

5. Aviation's role appears to be to establish facilities to handle many of the peripheral and statistical investigations to help fill in the background on electrostatics.

6. A distinction has to be made between electrostatic energy for propulsion and counterbary. Counterbary is the manipulation of gravitational force lines; barycentric control is the adjustment to such manipulative capability to produce a stable type of motion suitable for transportation.

7. Electrostatic energy sufficient to produce low speeds (a few thousand dynes) has already been demonstrated. Generation of a region of positive electrostatic energy on one side of a plate and negative on the other sets up the same lift or propulsion effect as the pressure and suction below and above a wing, excepts that in the case of electrostatic

32

application no airflow is necessary.

8. Electrostatic energy sufficient to produce a Mach 3 fighter is possible with megavolt energies and a k of over 10,000.

9. k figures of 6,000 have been obtained from some ceramic materials and there are prospects of 30,000.

10. Apart from electrogravitics there are other rewards from investment in electrostatic equipment. Automation, autonetics and even turbine development use similar laboratory facilities.

11. Progress in electrogravitics probably awaits a new genius in physics who can find a single equation to tie up all the conflicting observations and theory on the structure and arrangement of forces and the part the high energy particles play in the nucleus. This can occur any time, and the chances are improved now that Bev. energies[*] are being obtained in controlled laboratory conditions.

* * * *

---

[*] Ed. Note: Bev = billion electron volts which is now commonplace in physics experiments using particle accelerators in the 21st century.

APPENDIX I

EXTRACTS FROM AVIATION REPORT

ANTI-GRAVITATION RESEARCH

The basic research and technology behind electro-anti-gravitation is so much in its infancy that this is perhaps one field of development where not only the methods but the ideas are secret. Nothing therefore can be discussed freely at the moment. Very few papers on the subject have been prepared so far, and the only schemes that have seen the light of day are for pure research into rigs designed to make objects float around freely in a box. There are various radio applications, and aviation medicine departments have been looking for something that will enable them to study the physiological effects on the digestion and organs of an environment without gravity. There are however long term aims of a more revolutionary nature that envisage equipment that can defeat gravity.

Aviation Report 20 August 1954

MANAGERIAL POLICY FOR ANTI-GRAVITICS

The prospect of engineers devising gravity-defeating equipment - or perhaps it should be described as the creation of pockets of weightless environments - does suggest that as a long term policy aircraft constructors will be required to place even more emphasis on electro-mechanical industrial plant, than is now required for the transition from manned to unmanned weapons. Anti-gravitics work is therefore likely to go to companies with the biggest electrical laboratories and facilities. It is also apparent that anti-gravitics, like other advanced sciences, will be initially sponsored for its weapon capabilities. There are perhaps two broad ways of using the science - one is to postulate the design of advanced type projectiles on their best inherent capabilities, and the more critical parameters (that now constitutes the design limitation) can be eliminated by anti-gravitics. The other, which is a longer term plan, is to create an entirely new environment with longer term plan, is to create an entirely new environment with devices operating entirely under an anti-gravitic envelope.

Aviation Report 24 August 1954

THE GREATER THE EASIER

Propulsion and atomic energy trends are similar in one respect: the more incredible the long term capabilities are, the easier it is to attain them. It is strange that the greatest of nature's secrets can be harnessed with decreasing industrial effort, but greatly increasing mental effort. The Americans went through the industrial torture to produce tritium for the first thermonuclear experiment, but later both they and the Russians were able to achieve much greater results with the help of lithium 6 hydride.

The same thing is happening in aviation propulsion: the nuclear fuels are promising to be tremendously powerful in their effect, but excessively complicated in their application, unless there can be some means of direct conversion as in the strontium 90 cell. But lying behind and beyond the nuclear fuels is the linking of electricity to gravity, which is an incomparably more powerful way of harnessing energy than the only method known to human intellect at present - electricity and magnetism. Perhaps the magic of barium aluminum oxide will perform the miracle in propulsion that lithium 6 hydride has done in the fusion weapon.

Certainly it is a well-known material in dielectrics, but when one talks of massive-k, one means of course five figures. At this early stage it is difficult to relate k to Mach numbers with any certainty, but realizable k can, with some kinds of arithmetic, produce astounding velocities. They are achievable, moreover, with in terms of engineering, but the most hideous in terms of theory. Einstein's general theory of relativity is, naturally, an important factor, but some of the postulates appear to depend on the unified field theory, which cannot yet be physically checked because nobody knows how to do it. Einstein hopes to find a way of doing so before he dies.

Aviation Report 31 August 1954

GRAVITICS FORMULATIONS

All indications are that there has still been little cognizance of the potentialities of electrostatic propulsion and it will be a major undertaking to re-arrange aircraft plants to conduct large-scale research and development into novel forms of dielectric and to improve condenser efficiencies and to develop the novel type of materials used for fabrication of the primary structure. Some extremely ambitious theoretical programs have been submitted and work towards realization of a manned vehicle has begun. On the evidence, there are far more definite indications that the incredible claims are realizable than there was, for instance, in supposing that uranium fission would result in a bomb. At least it is known, proof positive, that motion, using surprisingly low k, is possible. The fantastic control that again is feasible, has not yet been demonstrated, but there is no reason to suppose the arithmetic is faulty, especially as it has already led to quite brisk example of actual propulsion. That first movement was indeed an historic occasion, reminiscent of the momentous day at Chicago when the first pile went critical, and the phenomenon was scarcely less weird. It is difficult to imagine just where a well-organized examination into long term gravitics prospects would end. Though a circular platform is electrostatically convenient, it does not necessarily follow that the requirements of control by differential changes would be the same. Perhaps the strangest part of this whole chapter is how the public managed to foresee the concept, though not of course the theoretical principles that gave rise to it, before physical tests confirmed that the mathematics was right. It is interesting also that there is no point of contact between the conventional science of aviation and the New: it is a radical offshoot with no common principles. Aerodynamics, structures, heat engines, flapping controls, and all the rest of aviation is part of what might be called the Wright Brothers era - even the Mach 2.5 thermal barrier piercers are still Wright Brothers concepts, in the sense that they fly and they stall, and they run out of fuel after a short while, and they defy the earth's pull for a short while. Thus this century will be divided into two parts - almost to the day. The first half belonged to the Wright Brothers who foresaw nearly all the basic issues in which gravity was the bitter foe. In part of the second half, gravity will be the great provider. Electrical energy, rather irrelevant for propulsion in the first half becomes a kind of catalyst to motion in the second half of the century.

Aviation Report 7 September 1954

ELECTRO-GRAVITICS PARADOX

Realization of electro-static propulsion seems to depend on two theoretical twists and two practical ones. The two theoretical puzzles are: first, how to make a condenser the center of a propulsion system, and second is how to link the condenser system with the gravitational field. There is a third problem, but it is some way off yet, which is how to manipulate kva for control in all three axes as well as for propulsion and lift. The two practical tricks are first how, with say a Mach 3 weapon in mind, to handle 50,000 kva within the envelope of a thin pancake of 35 feet in diameter and second how to generate such power from within so small a space. The electrical power in a small aircraft is more than in a fair sized community the analogy being that a single rocketjet can provide as much power as can be obtained from the Hoover Dam. It will naturally take as long to develop electro-static propulsion as it has taken to coax the enormous power outputs from heat engines. True there might be a flame in the electro-gravitic propulsion system, but it would not be a heat engine - the temperature of the flame would be incidental to the function of the chemical burning process.

The curious thing is that though electro-static propulsion is the antithesis of magnetism,[*] Einstein's unified field theory is an attempt to link gravitation with electro-magnetism. This all-embracing theory goes on logically from the general theory of relativity, that gives an ingenious geometrical interpretation of the concept of force which is mathematically consistent with gravitation but fails in the case of electro-magnetism, while the special theory of relativity is concerned with the relationship between mass and energy. The general theory of relativity fails to account for electro-magnetism because the forces are proportional to the charge and not to the mass. The unified field theory is one of a number of attempts that have been made to bridge this gap, but it is baffling to imagine how it could ever be observed. Einstein himself thinks it is virtually impossible. However Hlavaty claims now to have solved the equations by assuming that gravitation is a manifestation of electro-magnetism.

This being so it is all the more incredible that electro-static

---

[*]Though in a sense this is true, it is better expressed in the body of this report than it was here in 1954.

propulsion (with kva for convenience fed into the system and not self-generated) has actually been demonstrated. It may be that to apply all this very abstruse physics to aviation it will be necessary to accept that the theory is more important than this or that interpretation of it. This is how the physical constants, which are now regarded as among the most solid of achievements in modern physics, have become workable, and accepted. Certainly all normal instincts would support the Einstein series of postulations, and if this is so it is a matter of conjecture where it will lead in the long term future of the electro-gravitic science.

Aviation Report 10 September 1954

ELECTRO-GRAVITIC PROPULSION SITUATION

Under the terms of Project Winterhaven the proposals to develop electro-gravitics to the point of realizing a Mach 3 combat type disc were not far short of the extensive effort that was planned for the Manhattan District.[*] Indeed the drive to develop the new prime mover is in some respects rather similar to the experiments that led to the release of nuclear energy in the sense that both involve fantastic mathematical capacity and both are sciences so new that other allied sciences cannot be of very much guide. In the past two years since the principle of motion by means of massive-k was first demonstrated on a test rig, progress has been slow. But the indications are now that the Pentagon is ready to sponsor a range of devices to help further knowledge. In effect the new family of TVs would be on the same tremendous scope that was envisaged by the X-1, 2, 3, 4 and 5 and D.558s that were all created for the purpose of destroying the sound barrier -

---

[*]The proposals, it should be added, were not accepted.

which they effectively did, but it is a process that is taking ten solid years of hard work to complete. (Now after 7 years the X-2 has yet to start its tests and the X-3 is still in performance testing stage). Tentative targets now being set anticipate that the first disc should be complete before 1960 and it would take the whole of the sixties to develop it properly, even though some combat things might be available ten years from now.

One thing seems certain at this stage, that the companies likely to dominate the science will be those with the biggest computers to work out the ramifications of the basic theory. Douglas is easily the world's leader in computer capacity, followed by Lockheed and Convair. The frame incidentally is indivisible from the engine. If there is to be any division of responsibility it would be that the engine industry might become responsible for providing the electrostatic energy (by, it is thought, a kind of flame) and the frame maker for the condenser assembly which is the core of the main structure.

Aviation Report 12 October 1954

GRAVITICS STUDY WIDENING

The French are now understood to be pondering the most effective way of entering the field of electro-gravitic propulsion systems. But now least of the difficulties is to know just where to begin. There are practically no patents so far that throw very much light on the mathematics of the relation between electricity and gravity. There is, of course, a large number of patents on the general subject of motion and force, and some of these may prove to have some application.

There is, however, a series of working postulations embodied in the original Project Winterhaven, but no real attempt has been made in the working papers to go into the detailed engineering. All that had actually been achieved up to just

41

under a year ago was a series of fairly accurate extrapolations from the sketchy data that has so far been actually observed. The extrapolation of 50 mph to 1,800 mph, however, (which is what the present hopes and aspirations amount to) is bound to be a rather vague exercise. This explains American private views that nothing can be reasonable expected from the science yet awhile. Meanwhile, the NACA is active, and nearly all the Universities are doing work that borders close to what is involved here, and something fruitful is likely to turn up before very long.

Aviation Report 19 October 1954

GRAVITICS STEPS

Specification writers seem to be still rather stumped to know what to ask for in the very hazy science of electro-gravitic propelled vehicles. They are at present faced with having to plan the first family of things - first of these is the most realistic type of operational test rig, and second the first type of test vehicle. In turn this would lead to sponsoring of a combat disc. The preliminary test rigs which gave only feeble propulsion have been somewhat improved, but of course the speeds reached so far are only those more associated with what is attained on the roads rather than in the air. But propulsion is now known to be possible, so it is a matter of feeding enough KVA into condensers with better k figures. 50,000 is a magic figure for the combat saucer - it is this amount of KVA and this amount of k that can be translated into Mach 3 speeds.

Meanwhile Glenn Martin now feels ready to say in public that they are examining the unified field theory to see what can be done. It would probably be truer to say that Martin and other companies are now looking for men who can make

42

some kind of sense out of Einstein's equations. There's nobody in the air industry at present with the faintest idea of what it is all about. Also, just as necessary, companies have somehow to find administrators who know enough of the mathematics to be able to guess what kind of industrial investment is likely to be necessary for the company to secure the most rewarding prime contracts in the new science. This again is not so easy since much of the mathematics just cannot be translated into words. You either understand the figures, or you cannot ever have it explained to you. This is rather new because even things like indeterminacy in quantum mechanics can be more or less put into words.

Perhaps the main thing for management to bear in mind in recruiting men is that essentially electro-gravitics is a branch of wave technology and much of it starts with Planck's dimensions of action, energy and time, and some of this is among the most firm and least controversial sections of modern atomic physics.

Aviation Report 19 November 1954

ELECTRO-GRAVITICS PUZZLE

Back in 1948 and 49, the public in the U.S. had a surprisingly clear idea of what a flying saucer should, or could, do. There has never at any time been any realistic explanation of what propulsion agency could make it do those things, but its ability to move within its own gravitation field was presupposed from its manoeuvrability. Yet all this was at least two years before electro-static energy was shown to produce propulsion. It is curious that the public were so ahead of the empiricists on this occasion, and there are two possible explanations. One is that optical illusions or atmospheric phenomena offered a preconceived idea of how the ultimate aviation device ought to work. The other explanation might be that this was a recrudescence of Jung's theory of the Universal Mind which moves up and down in relation to the capabilities of the highest intellects and this may be a case of it reaching a very high peak of perception.

But for the air industries to realize and electro-gravitic aircraft means a return to basic principles in nuclear physics, and a re-examination of much in a wave technology that has hitherto been taken for granted. Anything that goes any way towards proving the unified field theory will have as great a bearing on electro-gravitics efforts as on the furtherance of nuclear power generally. But the aircraft industry might as well face up to the fact that priorities will in the end be competing with the existing nuclear science commitments. The fact that electro-gravitics has important applications other than for a weapon will however strengthen the case for governments to get in on the work going on.

Aviation Report 28 January 1955

MANAGEMENT NOTE FOR ELECTRO-GRAVITICS

The gas turbine engine produced two new companies in the U.S. engine field and they have, between them, at various times offered the traditional primes rather formidable competition. Indeed GE at this moment has, in the view of some, taken the Number Two position. In Britain no new firms managed to get a footing, but one, Metro-Vick, might have done if it had put its whole energies into the business. It is on the whole unfortunate for Britain that no bright newcomer has been able to screw up competition in the engine field as English Electric have done in the airframe business.

Unlike the turbine engine, electro-gravitics is not just a new propulsion system, it is a new made of thought in aviation and communications, and it is something that may become all-embracing. Theoretical studies of the science unfortunately have to extend right down to the mathematics of the meson and there is no escape from that. But the relevant facts wrung from the nature of the nuclear structure will have their impact on the propulsion system, the airframe and also its guidance. The airframe, as such, would not exist, and what is now a complicated stressed structure becomes some convenient form of hard envelope.

New companies therefore who would like to see themselves as major defence prime contractors in ten or fifteen years time are the ones most likely to stimulate development. Several typical companies in Britain and the U.S. come to mind - outfits like AiResearch, Raytheon, Plessey in England, Rotax and others. But the companies have to face a decade of costly research into theoretical physics and it means a great deal of trust. Companies are mostly overloaded already and they cannot afford it, but when they sit down and think about the matter they can scarcely avoid the conclusion that they cannot afford not to be in at the beginning.

Aviation Report 8 February 1955

ELECTRO-GRAVITICS BREAKTHROUGHS

Lawrence Bell said last week he thought that the tempo of development leading to the use of nuclear fuels and anti-gravitational vehicles (he meant presumably ones that create their own gravitational field independently of the earth's) would accelerate. He added that the breakthroughs now feasible will advance their introduction ahead of the time it has taken to develop the turbojet to its present pitch. Beyond the thermal barrier was a radiation barrier, and he might have added ozone poisoning and meteorite hazards, and beyond that again a time barrier. Time however is not a single calculable entity and Einstein has taught that an absolute barrier to aviation is the environmental barrier in which there are physical limits to any kind of movement from one point in space-time continuum to another. Bell (the company not the man) have a reputation as experimentalists and are not so earthy as some of the other U.S. companies; so while this first judgement on progress with electrogravitics is interesting, further word is awaited from the other major elements of the air business. Most of the companies are now studying several forms of propulsion without heat engines though it is early days yet to determine which method will see the light of day first. Procurement will open out because the capabilities of such aircraft are immeasurably greater than those envisaged with any known form of engine.

Aviation Report 15 July 1955

THERMONUCLEAR-ELECTROGRAVITICS INTERACTION

The point has been made that the most likely way of achieving the comparatively low fusion heat needed - 1,000,000 degrees provided it can be sustained (which it cannot be in fission for more than a microsecond or two of time) - is by use of a linear accelerator. The concentration of energy that may be obtained when accelerators are rigged in certain ways make the production of very high temperatures feasible but whether they could be concentrated enough to avoid a thermal heat problem remains to be seen. It has also been suggested that linear accelerators would be the way to develop the high electrical energies needed for creation of local gravitational systems. It is possible therefore to imagine that the central core of a future air vehicle might be a linear accelerator which would create a local weightless state by use of electrostatic energy and turn heat into energy without

46

chemical processes for propulsion. Eventually - towards the end of this century - the linear accelerator itself would not be required and a ground generating plant would transmit the necessary energy for both purposes by wave propagation.

Aviation Report 30 August 1955

POINT ABOUT THERMONUCLEAR REACTION REACTORS

The 20 year estimate by the AEC last week that lies between present research frontiers and the fusion reactor probably refers to the time it will take to tap fusion heat. But it may be thought that rather than use the molecular and chemical processes of twisting heat into thrust it would be more appropriate to use the new heat source in conjunction with some form of nuclear thrust producer which would be in the form of electrostatic energy. The first two Boeing nuclearjet prototypes now under way are being designed to take either molecular jets or nuclear jets in case the latter are held up for one reason or another. But the change from molecular to direct nuclear thrust production in conjunction with the thermonuclear reactor is likely to make the aircraft designed around the latter a totally different breed of cat. It is also expected to take longer than two decades, though younger executives in trade might expect to live to see a prototype.

Aviation Report 14 October 1955

ELECTROGRAVITICS FEASIBILITY

Opinion on the prospects of using electrostatic energy for propulsion, and eventually for creation of a local gravitational field isolated from the earth's has naturally polarized into the two opposite extremes. There are those who say it is nonsense from start to finish, and those who are satisfied from performance already physically manifest that it is possible and will produce air vehicles with absolute capabilities and no moving parts. The feasibility of a Mach 3 fighter (the present aim in studies) is dependent on a rather large k extrapolation, considering the pair of saucers that have physically demonstrated the principle only an achieved speed of some 30 fps. But, and this is important, they have attained a working velocity using a very inefficient (even by today's knowledge) form of condenser complex. These humble beginnings are surely as hopeful as Whittle's early postulations.

It was, by the way, largely due to the early references in Aviation Report that work is gathering momentum in the U.S. Similar studies are beginning in France, and in England some men are on the job full time.

Aviation Report 15 November 1955

ELECTRO-GRAVITICS EFFORT WIDENING

Companies studying the implications of gravitics are said, in a new statement, to include Glenn Martin, Convair, Sperry-Rand, Sikorsky, Bell, Lear Inc. and Clark Electronics. Other companies who have previously evinced interest include Lockheed, Douglas and Hiller. The remainder are not disinterested, but have not given public support to the new science - which is widening all the time. The approach in the U.S. is in a sense more ambitious than might have been expected. The logical approach, which has been suggested by Aviation Studies, is to concentrate on improving the output of electrostatic rigs in existence that are known to be able to provide thrust. The aim would be to concentrate on electrostatics for propulsion first and widen the practical engineering to include establishment of local gravity forcelines, independent of those of the earth's, to provide unfettered verticle movement as and when the mathematics develops.

However, the U.S. approach is rather to put money into fundamental theoretical physics of gravitation in an effort first to create the local gravitation field. Working rigs would follow in the wake of the basic discoveries. Probably the correct course would be to sponsor both approaches, and it is now time that the military stepped in with big funds. The trouble about the idealistic approach to gravity is that the aircraft companies do not have the men to conduct such work.

There is every expectation in any case that the companies likely to find the answers lie outside the aviation field. These would emerge as the masters of aviation in its broadest sense.

The feeling is therefore that a company like A.T.& T. is most likely to be first in this field. This giant company (unknown in the air and weapons field) has already revolutionized modern warfare with the development of the junction transistor and is expected to find the final answers to absolute vehicle levitation. This therefore is where the bulk of the sponsoring money should go.

Aviation Report 9 December 1955

APPENDIX II

ELECTROSTATIC PATENTS

ELECTROSTATIC MOTORS

(a) American patents still in force.

2,413,391	Radio Corp.America	20-6-42/31-12-46	Power Supply System
2,417,452	Ratheon Mfg.Co.	17-1-44/18- 3-47	Electrical System
2,506,472	W.B. Smith	3-7-46Holl/ 2- 5-50	Electrical Ignition Apparatus
2,545,354	G.E.C.	16-3-50/13- 3-51	Generator
(=Engl.P,678,953)			
2,567,373	Radio Corp.America	10-5-49/11- 9-51	El'static Generator
2,577,446	Chatham Electronics	5-8-50/ 4-12-51	El'static Voltage Generator
2,578,908	US-Atomic Energy C.,	26-5-47/18-12-51	El'static Voltage Generator
2,588,513	Radio Corp,America	10-6-49/11- 3-52	El'static High-Voltage Generator
2,610,994	Chatham Electronics	1-9-50/16- 9-52	El'static Voltage Generator
2,682,191	P.Okey	31-7-52/8 -12-53	El'static Machine
2,687,615	R.G. Brown	30-1-52/26- 1-54	El'static Generator
2,671,177	Consolidated Engg.Corp	4-8-51/2 - 3-54	El'static Charging App's.
2,701,844	H.R. Vasaop	8-1250/ 8- 2-55	El'static Generator of Electricty
2,702,353	US-Navy	17-7-52/15- 2-55	Miniature Printed Circuit Electrostatic Generator

(b) British patents still in force.

651,153	Metr.-Vickers Electr,Co.	20-5-48/14- 3-51	Voltage Transformation of electrical energy.
651,295	Ch.F.Warthen sr.(U.S.A.)	6-8-48/14- 3-51	Electrostatic A.C. Generator
731,776	"Licentia".	19-9-52 & 21-11-52Gr/15- 6-55	El'static High-Voltage Generator

(c) French patents still in force

753,353	H.Chaumat	19-7-32/13-10-33	Moteur électrostatique utilisant l'énergie cinétique d'ions gazeux
749,532	H.Chaumat	24-1-33/29- 7-33	Machine électrostatique à excitation indépendante

The following patents derive from F.Jolivet (Algiers), marked "A" and from
N.J.Felici, E.Gartner (Centre National des Recherches Scientifique - CRNS -)
later also by R.Morel, M.Point etc. (S.A. des Machines Electrostatiques -SAMES-)
and of Société d'Appareils de Contrôle et d'Equipement des Moteurs -SACEM-),
marked "G" (because the development was centred at the University Grenoble.

Mark of Applicant	Application Date	England	America	France.	Germany	Title
G	8-11-44) 14- 8-45)	637,434	2,486,140	993,017 56,027	860,649	Electrostatic Influence Machine
G	17-11-44	639,653	2,523,688	903,052	815,667	Electrostatic Influence Machine
A	28- 2-45			912,494		Inducteurs de Machines el'static
G	3- 3-45	643,660	2,519,554	995,442	832,596	El'static Machines
A	9- 6-45			915,929		Machines electrostatiques à flasques
A	16- 8-45			918,547		Generatrice el'statique.
G	20- 9-45) 21- 9-45)	643,664	2,523,689	998,397 56,356	837,267	Electrostatic Machines
A	4- 2-46			923,593		Generatrice el'statique
G	17- 7-46	643,879	2,530,193	1002,031	811,595	Generating Machines
G	20- 2-47	671,033	2,599,168			Ignition device
G	21-3 -47	655,474	2,542,494 Re-23,560	944,574	860,650	El'static Machines
G	6- 6-47	645,916	2,522,106	948,409	810,042	El'static Machines
A	16- 6-47			947,921		Generatrice él'statique
G	16- 1-48	669,645	2,540,327	961,210	810,043	El'static Machines
G	21- 1-49	669,454	2,617,970	907,991	815,566	El'static Machines
G	7- 2-49	675,649	2,649,566	1010,924	870,575	El'static Machines
G	15- 4-49	693,914	2,604,502	1011,902	832,634	Commutators for electrical machine
G	6-11-49	680,178	2,656,502	1004,950	850,485	El'static Generato
G	8-10-50) 20- 2-51)	702,494	2,675,516	1030,623		El'static Generate
G	29-11-50) 20- 2-51)	702,421		1028,596		El'static Generate
G	21-11-51	710,607		1051,430	F10421	El'static Machines
G	20- 8-52	731,773	2,702,869		938,198	El'static Machines
G	6-11-52	745,480				El'static Generator
G	12- 2-53	745,783				Rotating El'static Machines
G	8- 1-52	715,010	2,685,654	1047,591		Rotating El'static Machines producing a periodical discharge.
G	27- 2-54	Appl'n No. 5726/55				El'static Machines
G	8- 3-54	6790/55				El'static Machines
G	28- 1-55	2740/56				El'static Machines

NOTE:- ALL THE LISTED PATENTS ARE STILL IN FORCE

THE GRAVITICS SITUATION

December 1956

Gravity Rand Ltd.
66 Sloane Street
London S W 1

Theme of the science for 1956-1970:
SERENDIPITY

Einstein's view:
"It may not be an unattainable hope that some day a clearer knowledge of the processes of gravitation may be reached; and the extreme generality and detachment of the relativity theory may be illuminated by the particular study of a precise mechanism."

CONTENTS

53

Thanks to the Gravity Research Foundation for Appendix II to VI

I. Engineering note on present frontiers of knowledge

Gravitics is likely to follow a number of separate lines of development: the best known short term proposition is Townsend Brown's electrostatic propulsion by gravitators (details of which are to be found in the Appendix I). An extreme extrapolation of Brown's later rigs appears to suggest a Mach 3 interceptor type aircraft. Brown called this basically force and motion, but it does not appear to be the road to a gravitational shield or reflector. His is the brute force approach of concentrating high electrostatic charges along the leading edge of the periphery of a disk which yields propulsive effect. Brown originally maintained that his gravitators operate independently of all frames of references and it is motion in the absolute sense relative to the universe as a whole. There is however no evidence to support this. In the absence of any such evidence it is perhaps more convenient to think of Brown's disks as electrostatic propulsion which has its own niche in aviation. Electrostatic disks can provide lift without speed over a flat surface. This could be an important advance over all forms of airfoil which require induced flow; and lift without air flow is a development that deserves to be

54

followed up in its own right, and one that for military purposes is already envisaged by the users as applicable to all three services. This point has been appreciated in the United States and a program in hand may now ensure that development of large sized disks will be continued. This is backed up by the U.S. Government, but it is something that will be perused on a small scale. This acceptance follows Brown's original suggestion embodied in Project Winterhaven. Winterhaven recommended that a major effort be concentrated on electrogravitics based on the principle of his disks. The U.S. Government evaluated the disks wrongly, and misinterpreted the nature of the energy. This incorrect report was filed in an official assessment, and it took some three years to correct the earlier misconception. That brings development up to the fairly recent past, and by that time it was realized that no effort on the lines of Winterhaven was practical, and that more modest aims should be substituted. These were re-written around a new report which is apparently based on newer thoughts and with some later patents not yet published which form the basis of current U.S. policy. It is a matter of some controversy whether this research could be accelerated by more money but the impression in Gravity Rand is that the base of industry is perhaps more than adequately wide. Already companies are specializing in evolution of particular components of an electrogravitics disk. This implies that the science is in the same state as the ICBM namely that no new breakthroughs are needed, only intensive development engineering. This may be an optimistic reading of the situation, it is true that materials are now available for the condensers giving higher k figures than were postulated in Winterhaven as necessary, and all the ingredients necessary for the disks appear to be available. But industry is still some way from having an adequate power source, and possessing any practical experience of running such equipment.

The long term development of gravity shields, absorbers, and magic metals' appears at the moment however to be a basically different problem, and work in this is not being sponsored (officially, that is), so far as is known. The absorber or shield could be intrinsically a weapon of a great power, the limits of which are difficult to foresee. The power of device to undermine the electrostatic forces holding the atom together is a destructive by-product of military significance. In unpublished work Gravity Rand has indicated the possible effect of such a device for demolition. The likelihood of such work being sponsored in small countries outside the U.S. is slight, since there is general lack of money and resources and in all such countries quick returns are essential.

Many people hold that little or no progress can be made until the link in the Einstein unified field theory has been found. This is surely a somewhat defeatist view, because although no all-embracing explanation of the relationship between the extraordinary variety of high energy particles continually being uncovered is yet available much can be done to pin down the general nature of anti-gravity devices.

There are several promising approaches one of them is the search for negative mass, a second is to find a relationship between gravity and heat, and a third is to find the link between gravitation and the coupled particles. Taking the first of these: negative mass, the initial task is to prove the existence of negative mass, and Appendix II outlines how it might be done, this is Mozer's approach which is based on the Schroedinger time independent equation with the center of mass motion removed. As the paper shows this requires some 100 bev which is beyond the power of existing particle accelerators: however the present Russian and American nuclear program envisage 50 bev bevatrons within a few years and at the present rate of progress in the nuclear sciences it seems possible that the existence of negamass will be proved by this method of a Bragg analysis of the crystal structure or disproved. If negamass is established the precise part played by the subnuclear particles could be quickly determined. Working theories have been built up to explain how negative masses would be repelled by positive masses and pairs would accelerate gaining kinetic energy until they reach the speed of light and then assume the role of the high energy particles. It has been suggested by Ferrell that this might explain the role of neutrino, but this seems unlikely without some absence of rest mass or charge of the neutrino makes it especially intriguing. Certainly further study of the neutrino would be relevant to gravitational problems. If therefore the aircraft industry regards antigravity as part of its responsibilities it cannot escape the necessity of monitoring high-energy physics of the neutrino. There are two companies definitely doing this but little or no evidence that most of the others know even what a neutrino is.

The relationship between electrical charges and gravitational forces however will depend on the right deductions being drawn from excessively small abnormalities (see Appendix VI). First clues to such small and hitherto unnoticed effects will come by study of the unified field theory: such effects may be observed in work on the gravithermals, and interacting effects of heat and gravity. This as Beams says (see Appendix III) is due to results from the alignment of the atoms. Gravity tensions applied across the ends of a tube filled with electrolyte can produce heat or be used to furnish power. The logical extension of this is an absorber of gravity in the form of a flat plate and the gravitative flux acting on it (its atomic and molecular structure, its weight density and form are not at this stage clear) would lead to an increase in heat of the mass of its surface and subsurface particles.

The third approach is to aim at discovering a connection between nuclear particles and the gravitational field. This also returns to the need for interpreting microscopic relativistic phenomena at one extreme in terms of microscopic quantum mechanical phenomena at the other. Beaumont in suggesting a solution recalls how early theory established, rough and ready assumptions of the characteristics of electron spin before the whole science of the atomic orbital was worked out. These were based on observation, and they were used with some effect at a time when data was needed. Similar assumptions of complex spin might be used to link the microscopic to the macroscopic. At any rate there are some loose ends and complex spin to be tied up, and these could logically be sponsored with some expectation of results by companies wondering how to make a contribution.

If a real spin or rotation is applied to a planar geoid the gravitational equipotentials can be made less convex, plane or concave. These have the effect of adjusting the intensity of the gravitational field at will, which is a requirement for the gravity absorber. Beaumont seemed doubtful whether external power would have to be applied to achieve this but it seems reasonable to suppose that power could be fed into the system to achieve a beneficial adjustment to the gravitational field, and conventional engineering methods could ensure that the weightlessness from the spin inducer. The engineering details of this naturally still in the realms of conjecture but at least it is something that could be worked out with laboratory rigs, and again the starting point is to make more accurate observations of small effects. The technique would be to accept any anomalies in nature, and from them to establish what would be needed to induce a pin artificially.

It has been argued that the scientific community faces a seemingly impossible task in attempting to alter gravity when the force is set up by a body as large as this planet and that to change it might demand a comparable force of similar planetary dimensions. It was scarcely surprising therefore that experience had shown that while it has been possible to observe the effects of gravity it resisted any form of control or manipulation. But the time is fast approaching when for the first time it will be within the capability of engineers with bevatrons to work directly wit particles that, it is increasingly accepted contribute to the source of gravitation, and whilst that in itself may not lead to an absorber of gravity, it will at least throw more light on the sources of the power.

Another task is solution (see Appendix IV) of outstanding equations to convert gravitational phenomena to nuclear energy. The problem, still not yet solved, may support the Bondi-Hoyle theory that expansion of the universe represents energy continually annihilated instead of being carried to the boundaries of the universe. This energy loss manifests itself in the behavior of the heparin and K-particles which would, or might, form the link between the microcosm and macrocosm. Indeed Deser and Arnowitt propose that the new particles are a direct link between gravitationally produced energy and nuclear energy. If this were so it would be the place to begin in the search for practical methods of gravity-manipulation. It would be realistic to assume that the K-particles are such a link. Then a possible approach might be to disregard objections which cannot be explained at this juncture until further unified field links are established. As in the case of the spin and orbital theories, which were naive in the beginning, the technique might have to accept the apparent forces and make theory fit observation until more is known.

Some people feel that the chances of finding such a unified field theory to link gravity and electrodynamics are high yet think that the finding of a gravity shield is slight because of the size of the energy source, and because the chances of seeing unnoticed effect seem slender. Others feel the opposite and believe that a link between the Einstein general relativistic and Quantum Theory disciplines. Some hope that both discoveries may come together while a few believe that a partial explanation of both may come about the same time, which will afford sufficient knowledge of gravitational fields to perfect an interim type of absorber using field links that are available. This latter seems the more likely since it is already beginning to happen. There is not likely to be any sudden full explanation of the microcosm and macrocosm, but one strand after another joining them will be fashioned as progress is made towards quantizing the Einstein theory.

II. Management Note on the Gravitics Situation

The present anti-gravity situation as one of watching and waiting by the large aircraft prime contractors for lofting inventions or technological breakthroughs. Clarence Birdseye in one of his last utterances thought that an insulator might be discovered by accident by someone working on a quite different problem and in 500 years gravity insulators would be commonplace. One might go further than Birdseye and say that principles of the insulator would, by then, be fundamental to human affairs, it would be as basic to the society as the difference today between the weight of one metal and another. But at same time it would be wrong to infer from Birdseye a remark that a sudden isolated discovery will be the key to the science. The hardware will come at a time when the industry is ready and waiting for it. It will arrive after a long period of getting accustomed to thinking in terms of weightlessness and naturally it will appear after the feasibility of achieving it in one form or another has been established in theory. (But this does not mean that harnessed forces will be necessarily fully understood at the outset.)

The aim of companies at this stage must therefore surely be to monitor the areas of progress in the world of high energy physics which seem likely to lead to establishment of the foundations of anti-gravity. This means keeping a watchful eye on electrogravitics, magnetogravitics, gravitics-isotopes and electrostatics in various forms for propulsion or levitation. This is not at the present stage a very expensive business, and investment in laboratory man-hours is necessary only when a certain line of reasoning which may look promising comes to a dead-end for lack of experimental data or only when it might be worth running some laboratory tests to bridge a chase between one part of a theory and another, or in connecting two or more theories together. If this is right, anti-gravity is in a state similar to nuclear propulsion after the NEPA findings, yet before the ANP project got under way. It will be remembered that was the period when the Atomic Energy Commission sponsored odd things here and there that needed doing. But it would be misleading to imply that hardware progress on electrostatic disks is presently so far as nuclear propulsion was in that state represented by ANP. True the NEPA-men came to the conclusion that a nuclear-propelled aircraft of a kind could be built, but it would be only a curiosity. Even at the time of the Lexington and Whitman reports it was still some way from fruition, the aircraft would have been more than a curiosity but not competitive enough to be seriously considered.

It is not in doubt that work on anti-gravity is in the realm of the longer term future. One of the tests of virility of an industry is the extent to which it is so self confident of its position that it can afford to sponsor R&D which cannot promise a quick return. A closing of minds to anything except line of development that will provide a quick return to a sign of either a straitlaced economy or of a pure lack of prescience, (or both).

Another consideration that will play its part in managerial decision is that major turning points in anti-gravity work are likely to prove far removed from the tools of the aircraft engineer. A key instrument for example that may determine the existence of negamass and establish posimass negamass interaction is the super bevatron. It needs some 100 bev gammas on hydrogen to perform a Bragg analysis of the elementary particle structure by selective reflection to prove the existence of negamass. This value is double as much the new Russian bevatron under construction and it is 15 times as powerful as the highest particle accelerations in the Berkeley bevatron so far attained. Many people think that nothing much can be done until negamass has been observed. If industry were to adopt this approach it would have a long wait and a quick answer at the end. But the negamass-posimass theory can be further developed, and, in anticipation of its existence, means of using it in a gravitationally neutralized body could be worked out. This moreover is certainly not the only possible approach a breakthrough may well come in the interaction between gravitative action and heat. Theory at the moment suggests that if gravity could produce heat the effect is limited at the moment to a narrow range (see Appendix V). But the significant thing would be establishment of a principle.

History may repeat itself thirty years ago, and even as recently as the German attempts to produce nuclear energy in the war, nobody would have guessed that power would be unlocked by an accident at the high end of the atomic table. All prophecies of atomic energy were concerned with how quickly means of fusion could be applied at the low end. In anti-gravity work, and this goes back to Birdseye, it may be an unrelated accident that will be the means of getting into the gravitational age. It is a prime responsibility of management to be aware of possible ways of using theory to accelerate such a process. In other words <u>serendipity</u>.

It is a common thought in industry to look upon the nuclear experience as a precedent for gravity, and to argue that gravitics will similarly depend on the use of giant tools, beyond the capabilities of the air industry; and that companies will edge into the gravitational age on the coat tails of the Government, as industry has done, or is doing, in nuclear physics. But this over looks the point that the two sciences are likely to be different in their investment. It will not need a place like Hanford or Savannah River to produce a gravity shield or insulator once the know how has been established. As a piece of conceptual engineering the project is probably likely to be much more like a repetition of the turbine engine. It will be simple in its essence, but the detailed componentry will become progressively more complex to interpret in the form of a stable flying platform and even more intricate when it comes to applying the underlying principles to a flexibility of operating altitude ranging from low present flight speeds at one extreme to flight in a vacuum at the other, this latter will be the extreme test of its powers. Again the principle itself will function equally in a vacuum. Townsend Brown's saucers could move in a vacuum readily enough, but the supporting parts must also work in a vacuum. In practice they tend to give trouble, just as gas turbines bits and pieces start giving trouble in proportion to the altitude gained in flight.

But one has to see this rise in complexity with performance and with altitude attainment in perspective; eventually the most advanced capability may be attained with the most extremely simple configurations. As is usual however in physics developments the shortest line of progress is a geodesic, which may in turn lead the propulsion trade into many roundabout paths as being the shortest distance between aims and achievement.

But aviation business is understandably interested in knowing precisely how to recognize early discoveries of significance, and the Gravity Rand report is intended to array and outline some of the more promising lines. One suggestion frequently made is that propulsion and levitation may be only the last though most important of a series of others, some of which will have varying degrees of gravitic element in their constitution. It may be that the first practical application will be in the greater freedom of communications offered by the change, in wave technique that it implies. A second application is to use the wave technique for anti-submarine detection, either airborne or seaborne. This would combine the width of horizon in search radar with the underwater precision of Magnetic Airborne Detection, and indeed it may have the range of scatter transmissions. Chance discoveries in the development of this equipment may lead to the formulation of new laws which would define the relationship of gravity in terms of usable propulsion symbols. Exactly how this would happen nobody yet knows; and what industry and government can do at this stage is to explore all the possible applications simultaneously, putting pressure where results seem to warrant it.

In a paper of this kind it is not easy to discuss the details of the wave technique in communications, and the following are some of the theories, briefly stated which require no mathematical training to understand, which it would be worth management keeping an eye on. In particular watch should be made of quantitative tests on lofting, and beneficiation of material. Even quite small beneficiation ratios are likely to be significant. There are some lofting claims being made of 20% and more, and the validity of these will have to be weighed carefully. Needless to say much higher ratios than this will have to be attained. New high k techniques and extreme k materials are significant. High speeds in electrostatic propulsion of small discs will be worth keeping track of (by high speed one means hundreds of m.p.h.) and some of these results are beginning to filter through for general evaluation. Weight mass anomalies, new oil-cooled cables, interesting negavolt gimmicks, novel forms of electrostatic augmentation with hydrocarbon and on hydrocarbon fuels are indicative, new patents under the broadest headings of force and motion may have value, new electrostatic generator inventions could tip the scales and unusual ways of turning condensers inside-out, new angular propulsion ideas for barycentric control; and generally certain types of saucer configuration are valuable pointers to ways minds are working.

Then there is the personnel reaction to such developments. Managements are in the hands of their technical men, and they should beware of technical teams who are dogmatic at this stage. To assert electro-gravitics is nonsense is as unreal as to say it is practically extant. Management should be careful of men in their employ with a closed mind or even partially closed mind on the subject.

This is a dangerous age when not only is anything possible, but it is possible quickly a wise Frenchman once said, "You have only to live long enough to see everything and the reverse of everything" and that is true in dealing with very advanced high energy physics of this kind. Scientists are not politicians they can reverse themselves once with acclaim, twice even with impunity. They may have to do so in the long road to attainment of this virtually perfect air vehicle. It is so easy to get bogged down with problems of the present; and whilst policy has to be made essentially with the present in mind, and in aviation a conservative policy always pays, it is management's task and duty to itself to look as far ahead as the best of its technicians in assessing the posture of the industry.

III	GLOSSARY
Gravithermal	Alloy which may be heated or cooled by gravity waves (Lover's definition)
Thermistors: Electrade:	Materials capable of being influenced by gravity
Gravitator:	A plurity of cell units connected in series:negative and positive electrodes with an interposed insulating member. (Townsend Brown's definition)
Lofting:	The action of levitation where gravity's force is more than overcome by electrostatic or other propulsion.
Beneficiation	The treatment of an alloy or substance to leave it with an improved mass weight ratio
Counterbary:	This apparently is another name for lofting
Barycentric control	The environment for regulation of lofting processes in a vehicle.
Modulation:	The contribution to lofting conferred on a vehicle b treatment of the substance of its construction as distinct from that added to it by outside forces
Absorber; insulator	These terms, there is no formal distinction between them yet, are based on an analogy with electromagnetism This is a questionable assumption since the similarity between electromagnetic and gravitational fields is valid only in some respects such as both having electric and magnetic elements. But the difference in coupling strengths, noted by many experimenters is fundamental to the science. Gravity moreover may turn out to be the only nonquantized field in nature, which would make it basically unique. The borrowing of

	terms from the field of electromagnetism is therefore only a temporary convenience. Lack of Cartesian representation makes this a baffling science for many people.
Negamass:	Proposed mass that inherently has a negative mass
Posimass:	Mass that observed quantity positively charged
Shield:	A device which not only opposes gravity (such as an absorber) but also furnishes an essential path along which or through which, gravity can act. Thus, whereas absorbers, reflectors and insulators can provide a gravitationally neutralized body, a shield would enable a vehicle or sphere to fall away, in proportion to the quantity of shielding material.
Screeing:	Gravity screeing was implied by Lanczos. It is the result of any combination of electric or magnetic field in which one or both elements are not subject to varying permeability in matter
Reflector:	A device consisting of material capable of generating buoyant forces which balance the force of attraction. The denser the material the greater the buoyancy force. With the density of the medium the result will be gravitationally neutralized. A greater density of material assumes a lofting role.
Electro-gravitics:	The application of modulating influences in an electrostatic propulsion system.
Magneto-gravitics:	The influence of electromagnetic and meson fields in a reflector

Boson fields:	These are defined as gravitational electromagnetic and meson fields (Metric tensor)
Fermion Fields:	These are electrons, neutrinos, nucleons and V particles (Spinors)
Gravitator cellular body:	Two or more gravitator cells connected in series within a body (Townsend Brown's definition)

REFERENCES

Mackenzie **Physical Review,** 2 pp. 321-43.

Eotvos, Pekar and Fekete, **Annalen der Physik** 68. (1922) pp.11-16.

Heyl, Paul R. **Scientific Monthly**. 47. (1938) p. 115.

Austin, Thwing, **Physical Review** 5, (1897), pp. 494-500.

Shaw, **Nature** (April 8, 1922) p. 462. Proc. Roy. Soc. 102, (Oct. 6, 1922), p. 46.

Brush, **Physical Review,** 31, p. 1113 (A).

Wold, **Physical Review**, 35, p. 296 (Abstract).

Majorana, **Attidella Reale, Accademie die Lincei**, 28, (1919), pp.160, 221, 313, 416, 480, 29 (1920) pp. 23, 90, 163, 235, Phil Mag. 39. (1920) p. 288.

Schneiderov, **Science**, (May 7, 1943), 97, sup. p. 10.

Brush, **Physical Review** 32, P. 633, (abstract).

Lanczos, **Science,** 74, (Dec. 4, 1931) sup. p. 10.

Eddington, **Report on the Relativity Theory of Gravitation** (1920) Fleetway Press, London.

W.D. Fowler et al, **Phys. Rev**. 93, 861, 1954.

R.L. Arnowitt and S. Deser, **Phys. Rev** 92 1061, 1953.

R.L. Arnowitt, **Bull, APS** 94 798. 1954 S. Deser, **Phys. Rev.** 93, 612, 1954.

N. Schein, D.M. Haskin and R.G. Glasser. **Phys. Rev.** 95, 855, 1954.

R.L. Arnowitt and S. Deser. unpublished Univ. of California Radiation Laboratory Report, 1954.

H. Bondi and T. Gold, **Mon. Not. R. Astr. Soc.** 108, 252, 1948

F. Hoyle, **Mon. Not. R. Astr. Soc.** 108, 372, 1948.

B.S. DeWitt. New Directions for Research in the Theory of Gravitation, **Essay on Gravity**, 1953.

C.H. Bondi. **Cosmology,** Cambridge University Press, 1952.

F.A.E. Pirani and A. Schild, **Physical Review** 79, 986 (1950)

Bergman, Penfield, Penfield Schiller and Zatzkis, **Phys. Rev.** 80, 81 (1950).

B.S. DeWitt. **Physical Review** 85, 653 (1952).

See, for example D. Boh, **Quantum Theory,** New York, Prentice-Hall, Inc., (1951) Chapter 22.

A. Pais, **Proceedings of the Lorentz Kamerlingh Onnes Conference,** Leyden, June 1953.

For the treatment of spinors in a unified field theory see W. Pauli. **Annalen der Physik,** 18, 337 (1933) See also B.S. DeWitt and C.M. DeWitt, **Physical Review,** 87, 116 (1952).

Carter, F.L., The Quantum Mechanical Electromagnetic Approach to Gravity, **Essay on Gravity** 1953.

On Negative mass in the Theory of Gravitation Prof. J. M. Luttinger **Essay on Gravity** 1951.

APPENDIX

SUMMARY OF TOWNSEND BROWN'S ORIGINAL PATENT SPECIFICATION*

This invention relates to a method of controlling gravitation and for deriving power therefrom, and to a method of producing linear force or motion. The method is fundamentally electrical.

The invention also relates to machines or apparatus requiring electrical energy that control or influence the gravitational field or the energy of gravitation; also to machines or apparatus requiring electrical energy that exhibit a linear force or motion which is believed to be independent of all frames of reference save that which is at rest relative to the universe taken as a whole, and said linear force or motion is furthermore believed to have no equal and opposite reaction that can be observed by any method commonly known and accepted by the physical science to date.

Such a machine has two major parts A and B. These parts may be composed of any material capable of being charged electrically. Mass A and mass B may be termed electrodes A and B respectively. Electrode A is charged negatively with respect to electrode B, or what is substantially the same, electrode B is charged positively with respect to electrode A, or what is usually the case, electrode A has an excess of

---

* Ed. Note: This is the disclosure (text) part of T. T. Brown's 1928 British patent #300,311, which is reprinted in its entirety in the Appendix of this book, with all of the diagrams, for your convenience.

electrons while electrode B has an excess of protons.

While charged in this manner the total force of A toward B is the sum of force g (due to the gravitational field), and force e (due to the imposed electrical field) and force x (due to the resultant of the unbalanced gravitational forces caused by the electro-negative charge or by the presence of an excess of electrons of electrode A and by the electro-positive charge or by the presence of an excess of protons on electrode B).

By the cancellation of similar and opposing forces and by the addition of similar and allied forces the two electrodes taken collectively possess a force 2x in the direction of B. This force 2x, shared by both electrodes, exists as a tendency of these electrodes to move or accelerate in the direction of the force, that is, A toward B and B away from A. Moreover any machine or apparatus possessing electrodes A and B will exhibit such a lateral acceleration or motion if free to move.

In this specification, I have used terms as "gravitator cells" and gravitator cellular body" which are words of my own coining in making reference to the particular type of cell I employ in the present invention. Wherever the construction involves the use of a pair of electrodes, separated by an insulating plate or member, such construction complies with the term gravitator cells, and when two or more gravitator cells are connected in series within a body, such will fall within the meaning of gravitator cellular body The electrodes A and B are shown as having placed between them an insulating plate or member C of suitable material, such that the minimum number of electrons or ions may successfully penetrate it. This constitutes a cellular gravitator consisting of one gravitator cell.

It will be understood that, the cells being spaced substantial distance apart, the separation of adjacent positive and negative elements of separate cells is greater than the separation of the positive and negative elements of any cell and the materials of which the cells are formed being the more readily affected by the phenomena underlying my invention than the mere space between adjacent cells, any forces existing between positive and negative elements of adjacent cells can never become of sufficient magnitude to neutralize or balance the force created by the respective cells adjoining said spaces. The uses to which such a motor, wheel, or rotor may be put are practically limitless as can be readily understood without further description. The structure may suitably be called a gravitator motor of cellular type.

In keeping with the purpose of my invention an apparatus may employ the electrodes A and B within a vacuum tube. Electrons, ions, or thermions can migrate readily from A to B. The construction may be appropriately termed an electronic, ionic, or thermionic gravitator as the case may be.

In certain of the last named types of gravitator units, it is desirable or necessary to heat to incandescence the whole or a part of electrode A to obtain better emission of negative thermions or electrons or at least to be able to control that emission by variation in the temperature of said electrode A. Since such variations also influence the magnitude of the longitudinal force or acceleration exhibited by the tube, it proves to be a very convenient method of varying this effect and of electrically controlling the motion of the tube. The electrode A may be heated to incandescence in any convenient way as by the ordinary methods utilizing electrical resistance or electrical induction.

Moreover, in certain types of the gravitator units, now being considered, it is advantageous or necessary also to conduct away from the anode or positive electrode B excessive heat that may be generated during the operation. Such cooling is effected externally by means of air or water cooled flanges that are in thermo connection with the anode, or it is effected internally by passing a stream of water, air, or other fluid through a hollow anode made specially for that purpose.

The gravitator motors may be supplied with the necessary electrical energy for the operation and resultant motion thereof from sources outside and independent of the motor itself. In such instances they constitute external or independently excited motors. On the other hand the motors when capable of creating sufficient power to generate by any method whatsoever all the electrical energy required therein for the operation of said motors are distinguished by being internal or self-excited. Here, it will be understood that the energy created by the operation of the motor may at times be vastly in excess of the energy required to operate the motor. In some instances the ratio may be even as high as a million to one. Inasmuch as any suitable means for supplying the necessary electrical energy, and suitable conducting means for permitting the energy generated by the motor to exert the expected influences on the same may be readily supplied, it is now deemed necessary to illustrate details herein. In said self-excited motors the energy necessary to overcome the friction or other resistance in the physical structure of the apparatus, and even to accelerate the motors against such resistance, is believed to be derived solely from the gravitational field or the energy of gravitation. Furthermore, said acceleration in the self-excited gravitator motor can be harnessed mechanically so as to produce usable energy or power, said usable energy or power, as aforesaid, being derived from or transferred by the apparatus solely from the energy of gravitation.

The gravitator motors function as a result of the mutual and unidirectional forces exerted by their charged electrodes. The direction of these forces and the resultant motion thereby produced are usually toward to positive electrode. This movement is practically linear. It is this primary action with which I deal.

As has already been pointed out herein, there are two ways in which this primary action can accomplish mechanical work. First, by operating in a linear path as it does naturally, or second, by operating in a circular path. Since the circle is the most easily applied of all the geometric figures, it follows that the rotary form is the most important.

There are three general rules to follow in the construction of such motors. First, the insulating sheets should be as thin as possible and yet have a relatively high puncture voltage. It is advisable also to use paraffin saturated insulators on account of their high specific resistance. Second, the potential difference between any two metallic plates should be as high as possible and yet be safely under the minimum puncture voltage of the insulator. Third, there should in most cases be as many plates as possible in order that the saturation voltage of the system might be raised well above the highest voltage limit upon which the motor is operated. Reference has previously been made to the fact that in the preferred embodiment of the invention herein disclosed the movement is towards the positive electrode. However, it will be clear that motion may be had in a reverse direction determined by what I have just termed saturation voltage by which is meant the efficiency peak or maximum of action for that particular type of motor: the theory, as I may describe it, being that as the voltage is increased, the force or action increases to a maximum which represent the greatest action in a negative to positive direction. If the voltage were increased beyond that maximum the action would decrease to zero and thence to the positive to negative direction.

The rotary motor comprises broadly speaking, an assembly of a plurality of linear motors fastened to or bent around the circumference of a wheel. In that case the wheel limits the action of the linear motors to a circle, and the wheel rotates in the manner of a fireworks pin wheel.

I declare that what I claim is:

1. A method of producing force or motion which comprises the step of aggregating the predominating gravitational lateral or linear forces of positive and negative charges which are so cooperatively related as to eliminate or practically eliminate the effect of the similar and opposing forces which said charges exert.

2. A method of producing force or motion, in which a mechanical or structural part is associated with at least two electrodes or the like, of which the adjacent electrodes or the like have charges of differing characteristics, the resultant, predominating, unidirectional gravitational force of said electrodes or the like being utilized to produce linear force or motion of said part.

3. A method according to Claim 1 or 2, in which the predominating force of the charges or electrodes is due to the normal gravitational field and the imposed electrical field.

4. A method according to Claim 1, 2 or 3, in which the electrodes or other elements bearing the charges are mounted, preferably rigidly, on a body or support adapted to move or

exert force in the general direction of alignment of the electrodes or other charge bearing elements.

5. A machine or apparatus for producing force or motion, which includes at least two electrodes or like elements adapted to be differently charged, so relatively arranged that they produce a combined linear force or motion in the general direction of their alignment.

6. A machine according to Claim 5 in which the electrodes or like elements are mounted, preferably rigidly on a mechanical or structural part, whereby the predominating uni-directional force obtained from the electrodes or the like is adapted to move said part or to oppose forces tending to move it counter to the direction in which it would be moved by the action of the electrodes or the like.

7. A machine according to Claim 5 or 6, in which the energy necessary for charging the electrodes or the like is obtained either from the electrodes themselves or from an independent source.

8. A machine according to Claim 5, 6 or 7, whose force action or motive power depends in part on the gravitational field or energy of gravitation which is controlled or influenced by the motion of the electrodes or the like.

9. A machine according to any of Claim 5 to 8, in the form of a motor including a gravitator cell or a gravitator cellular body, substantially as described.
10. A machine according to Claim 9, in which the gravitator cellular body or an assembly of the gravitator cells is mounted on a wheel-like support, whereby rotation of the latter may be effected, said cells being of electronic, ionic or

thermionic type.

11. A method of controlling or influencing the gravitational field or the energy of gravitation and for deriving energy or power therefrom comprising the use of at least two masses differently electrically charged, whereby the surrounding gravitational field is affected or distorted by the imposed electrical field surrounding said charged masses, resulting in a uni-directional force being exerted on the system of charged masses in the general direction of the alignment of the masses, which system when permitted to move in response to said force in the above mentioned direction derives and accumulates as the result of said movement usable energy or power from the energy of gravitation or the gravitational field which is so controlled, influenced, or distorted.

12. The method of and the machine or apparatus for producing force or motion, by electrically controlling or influencing the gravitational field or energy of gravitation.

APPENDIX II

A Quantum Approach To the Existence of Negative Mass and Its Utilization in the Construction of Gravitationally Neutralized Bodies.

Since the overwhelming majority of electrostatic quantum mechanical effects rely for their existence on an interplay of attractive and repulsive forces arising from two types of charge, few if any fruitful results could come from a quantum mechanical investigation of gravity unless there should be two types of mass. The first type, positive mass (hereafter denoted as posimass) retains all the properties attributed to ordinary mass, while the second type, negative mass (hereafter noted as negamass) differs only in that its mass is an inherently negative quantity.

By considering the quantum mechanical effects of the existence of these two types of mass, a fruitful theory of gravity will be developed. Theory will explain why negamass has never been observed, and will offer a theoretical foundation to experimental methods of detecting the existence of negamass and utilizing it in the production of gravitationally neutralized bodies.

To achieve these results recourse will be made to Schroedinger's time-independent equation with the center of mass motion removed. This equation is:

$$-h^2/2\mu \, \nabla^2 \, \psi + V \, \psi = E \, \psi$$

where all the symbols represent the conventional quantum mechanical quantities. Particular attention will be paid to the reduced mass:

$$\mu = \frac{m_1 \, m_2}{m_1 + m_2}$$

where m_1 and m_2 are the masses of the two interacting bodies.

One can approach the first obstacle that any theory of negamass faces, namely the explanation of why negamass has never been observed, by a consideration of how material bodies would be formed if a region of empty space were suddenly filled with many posimass and negamass quanta. To proceed along these lines, one must first understand the nature of the various possible quantum mechanical interactions of posimass and negamass.

Inserting the conventional gravitational interaction potential into Schroedinger's equation and solving for the wave function ψ, yields the result that the probability of two posimass quanta being close together is greater than the possibility of their being separated. Hence, there is said to be an attraction between pairs of posimass quanta. By a similar calculation it can be shown that while the potential form is the same, two negamass quanta repel each other. This arises from the fact that the reduced mass term in Schroedinger's equation is negative in this latter case. The type of posimass-negamass interaction is found to depend on the relative sizes of the masses of the interacting posimass and negamass quanta, being repulsive if the mass of the negamass quantum is greater in absolute value than the mass of the posimass quantum, and attractive in the opposite case. If the two masses are equal in absolute value, the reduced mass is infinite and Schroedinger's equation reduces to:

$$(V - E) \psi = 0$$

Since the solution $\psi = 0$ is uninteresting physically, it must be concluded that $V = E$, and hence there is no kinetic energy of relative motion. Thus, highest energy state. Thus, independent of, and in addition to the attractive posimass-posimass gravitational interaction there is a repulsive quantum mechanical exchange interaction between pairs of posimass quanta, when the system is in state E_{odd}. The result of these two oppositely directed interactions is the two posimass quanta are in stable equilibrium at some separation distance. Since this equilibrium occurs between all posimass pairs in an elementary particle, a necessary consequence of the existence of negamass is that when in the first excited state elementary particles have a partial crystalline structure.

This theoretical conclusion is capable of experimental verification by performing a Bragg analysis of the elementary particle structure through shining high energy gamma rays on hydrogen. Part of the gamma ray energy will be utilized in lowering the system from energy E_{even} to E_{odd}, and if selective reflection is observed, it will constitute a string verification of the existence of negamass. An order of magnitude calculation shows that, if the equilibrium distance between pairs of posimass quanta is one one millionth the radius of an electron, 100 bev gamma rays will be required to perform this experiment.

Having discussed why negamass has never been observed, and having derived an experimental test of its existence, it is next desirable to develop an experimental method utilizing negamass in the production of gravitationally neutralized bodies by further consideration of some ideas previously advanced. It has been pointed out that if a source of negamass is present, a posimass sphere continues to absorb negamass quanta until equilibrium is reached as a result of the reduced mass becoming infinite. Because the sphere thus produced is practically massless, and because the gravitational interaction between two bodies is proportional to the product of their respective masses, it follows that the sphere is practically unaffected by the presence of other bodies. And thus the problem of making gravitationally neutralized bodies is reduced to the problem of procuring a source of negamass quanta. This will be the next problem discussed.

The binding energy of a negamass quantum in a posimass sphere may be obtained as one of the eigenvalue solutions to Schroedinger's Equation. If the negamass quanta in a body are excited to energies in excess of this binding energy by shining sufficient energetic gamma rays on the body, these negamass quanta will be emitted and a negamass source will thus be obtained.

To estimate the gamma ray energy required to free a negamass quantum from a posimass body, certain assumptions must be made concerning the size and mass of a posimass and negamass quanta. Since these quantities are extremely indefinite, and since the whole theory is at best qualitative, attempting to estimate the energy would be a senseless procedure. Suffice it to that because of the intimate sub-elementary nature of the posimass-negamass interaction, it seems reasonable to assume that quite energetic gamma rays will be required to break this strong bond.

To briefly review what has been shown, a quantum mechanical theory of negamass has been developed, based on the assumptions that gravitational interactions obey the laws of quantum mechanics and that all possible interactions of negamass and posimass with themselves and each other follow the well known inverse square law. This theory explains the experimental fact that negamass has never been observed, and outlines plausible experimental methods of determining the existence of negamass and utilizing it in the construction of gravitationally neutralized bodies. While these experimental methods may perhaps be put on the realm of

82

practicality at the present, there is every reason to hope that they will be performable in the future. At the time, the while there is an interaction potential between the equal mass posimass and negamass quanta, it results in no relative acceleration and thus, no mutual attraction or repulsion. While much could be said about the philosophical implications of the contradiction between this result and Newton's 2nd Law, such discussion is out of the scope of the present paper, and the author shall, instead, return with the above series of derivations to a consideration on the construction of material bodies in a region suddenly filled with many posimass and negamass quanta.

Because of the nature of posimass-posimass and negamass-negamass interactions, the individual posimass quanta soon combine into small posimass spheres, while nothing has, as yet, united any negamass quanta. Since it is reasonable to assume that a posimass sphere weighs more than a negamass quantum in absolute value, it will attract negamass quanta and begin to absorb them. This absorption continues until the attraction between a sphere and the free negamass quanta becomes zero due to the reduced mass becoming infinite. The reduced mass becomes infinite when the sphere absorbs enough posimass and negamass quanta equal to the negative of the mass of the next incoming negamass quantum. Thus, the theory predicts that all material bodies after absorbing as many negamass quanta as they can hold, weigh the same very small amount regardless of size.

Since this prediction is in violent disagreement with experimental fact, one must conclude that the equilibrium arising as a result of the reduced mass becoming infinite has not yet been reached. That is, assuming that negamass exists at all, there are not enough negamass quanta present in the universe to allow posimass spheres to absorb all the negamass they can hold. One is thus able to explain the experimental fact that negamass has never been observed by deriving the above mechanism in which the smaller amounts of negamass that may be present in the universe are strongly absorbed by the greater amounts of posimass, producing bodies composed of both posimass and negamass, but which have a net positive, variable, total mass.

Having thus explained why negamass has never been observed in the pure state, it is next desirable to derive an experimental test if the existence of negamass through considering the internal quantum mechanical problem of small amounts of negamass in larger posimass spheres. One is able to gain much physical insight into this problem by simplifying it to the qualitatively similar problem of one negamass quantum in the field of two posimass quanta that are fixed distances apart. Further simplification from three dimensions to one dimension and replacement of the posimass quanta potentials by square barriers, yields a solution in which the ground state energy E_o of the negamass quantum in the field of one posimass quantum, is split into two energy levels in the field of the two posimass quanta. These two levels correspond to even and odd parity solutions of the wave equation where E lies higher and E_{odd} lower than E_o. The magnitudes of the differences E_{even} E_o and E_o E_{odd} depend on the separation distance between the two posimass quanta, being zero for infinite separation and increasing as this separation distance is decreased.

Since the energy of a system involving negamass tends

to a maximum in the most stable quantum mechanical configuration, the negamass quantum will normally be in state E_{even}. When the system is excited into state E_{odd} the negamass quantum will favor the situation in which the two posimass quanta are as far apart as possible, since E_{odd} increases with increasing separation distance between the two posimass quanta, and the system tends towards the plausibility of the existence of negamass and the theory behind the construction of gravitationally neutralized bodies from it, will meet their final tests.

SUMMARY PARAGRAPH

A quantum mechanical theory of negative mass is developed based on the assumption that gravitational interactions obey the laws of quantum mechanics, and that all possible interactions of negative and positive mass with themselves and each other follow the well known inverse square law. This theory explains the experimental fact that negative mass has never been observed, and outlines plausible experimental methods of determining the existence of negamass and utilizing it in the construction of gravitationally neutralized bodies.

Prof. F. Mozer

GRAVITY EFFECTS

The order of magnitude of the heat given off by an alloy as a result of the separation by gravity tension can be reliably estimated. Suppose we assume that an alloy of half tin and half lead completely fills a tube 5 meters long and 100 cm^2 cross section which is maintained accurately at a temperature 277°C. At this temperature the alloy is liquid. Suppose next that the tube is raised from a horizontal plane into a vertical position 1.c to a position where its length is parallel to the direction of gravity. If then the alloy is free from convection as it would be if it is maintained at uniform temperature and if it is held in this position for several months, the percentage of tin at the bottom of the tube will decrease while the relative amount at the top will increase. A simple calculation shows that the concentration of tin at the top is about one tenth of one percent greater than at the bottom and that approximately one calorie of heat is given off in the separation progress. If after several months the tube is again placed so that its length is in a horizontal plane, the tin and lead will remix due to the thermal agitation of the atoms and heat is absorbed by the alloy.

Another interesting effect occurs when an electrolyte is subjected to gravity tension. Suppose a five meter glass tube is filled with a water solution of say barium chloride and the electrical potential between its ends is measured first when the length of the tube is parallel to the horizontal and second, when its length is practically zero when the tube is horizontal and approximately eighty five microvolts when it is vertical. This effect was discovered be Des Coudres in 1892. If a resistor is attached across the ends when the tube is vertical, heat of course is produced. If the tube is maintained at constant temperature the voltage decreases with time and eventually vanishes. The effect is believed to result from the fact that the positively charged barium ions settle faster than the lighter negatively charged chlorine ions as a result of gravity tension.

In conclusion we have seen that gravity tension effects an alloy in such a way that it gives off heat. This phenomenon results from the alignment of the atoms and from their separation by the gravitational field, the contribution of the latter being larger than that of the former. Also the gravity tension sets up a potential across the ends of a tube filled with an electrolyte and this potential when applied across an external circuit may produce heat or drive an electric motor to furnish power. Several other small thermal effects possibly may arise from gravity tension in addition to those discussed above but space is not available to consider them in this essay. Also studies of the effect of gravitational fields and their equivalent centrifugal fields upon matter will no doubt be of great value in the future.

J.W. Beams

A LINK BETWEEN GRAVITATION AND NUCLEAR ENERGY

More quantitatively we propose the following field equations describing the above phenomena:

$$-kT_{\mu\nu} = R_{\mu\nu} + \tfrac{1}{2}Rg_{\mu\nu} + C_{\mu\nu}[\Phi,\Psi]$$

$$\left[\tfrac{1}{i}\gamma^{\mu}\partial_{j\mu} + m + \lambda\sigma^{\mu\nu}K_{\mu\nu}(x)\right]\Psi = 0$$

with a similar equation for Φ. In the above, Ψ represents the hyperon wave functions, and Φ the K-particle quantized field operators. The first three terms in the first equation are the usual structures in the Einstein General Relativity. The last term, $C_{\mu\nu}$, is the "creation" tensor[8] which is to give us our conversion from gravitational to nuclear energy. It is like $T_{\mu\nu}$ in being an energy-momentum term. In the second equation $\partial_{j\mu}$ represents the covariant derivative while γ^{μ} is a generalized Dirac matrix arranged so that the second equation is indeed covariant under the general group of coordinate transformations. The $\sigma^{\mu\nu}K_{\mu\nu}$ term will automatically include the higher hyperon levels. $C_{\mu\nu}$ is a functional of the hyperon and K-field variables Ψ and Φ. As can be seen these equations are coupled in two ways: first the creation term $C_{\mu\nu}$ depends upon the field variables Ψ and Φ while the gravitational metric tensor $g_{\mu\nu}$ enters through the covariant, derivative, *etc.* λ is a new universal constant giving the scale of the level spacings of the hyperons. Rigorously speaking the field equations should be, of course, second quantized. For purposes of obtaining a workable first approximation it is probably adequate to take expectation values and solve the semi-classical equations. The creation tensor $C_{\mu\nu}$, must be a bilinear integral of the Φ and Ψ fields and may have cross terms as well of the form $\int \Phi\overline{\Psi}\Psi(dx)$. These equations will indeed be difficult to solve, but upon solution will give the distribution of created energy and hence lead eventually to the more practical issues desired.

Stanley Deser and Richard Arnowitt

GRAVITY/HEAT INTERACTION

Let us suppose that we have to investigate the question whether gravitative action alone upon some given substance or alloy can produce heat. We do not specify its texture, density nor atomic structure. We assume simply the flux of gravitative action followed by an increase of heat in the alloy.

If we assume a small circular surface on the alloy then the gravitative flux on it may be expressed by Gauss' Theorem and it is $4 \pi M$, where M represents the mass of all sub-surface particles. The question is, can this expression be transformed into heat. We will assume it can be. Now recalling the relativity law connecting mass and energy:

$$M = m_o + T/c^2 \qquad \text{(by Einstein)}$$

where: T = kinetic energy
m_o = initial mass
c = velocity of light

we set

$$4 \pi M = m_o + \frac{m_o v^2}{2 c^2}$$

But v^2/c^2 is a proper fraction; hence $M = m_o + m_o/2k$

In the boundary case $v = c$, then $M = m_o (1 + 1/k)$.

For all other cases, $4\pi M = m_o \left(\dfrac{k+1}{k} \right)$ where $k \neq 0$

Strictly, M should be preceded by a conversion factor $1/k$ but if inserted, it does not alter the results. Thus if gravity could produce heat, the effect is limited to a narrow range, as this result shows.

It merits stress that in a gravitational field the flow lines of descent are Geodesics.

J. Wickenden

WEIGHT-MASS ANOMALY

There is a great need for a precise experimental determination of the weight to mass ratio of protons or electrons. Since the ratio for a proton plus an electron is known already, the determination of the ratio for either particle is sufficient. The difficulty of a direct determination of the gravitational deflection of a charged particle in an experiment similar to the neutron or neutral atom experiment is due to electrical forces being much greater than gravitational field forces. Thus stray electrons or ions which are always present on the walls of an apparatus can exert sufficient force to completely mask the gravitational force. Even if the surface charges are neglected, image charges of the electron beam itself and self-repulsion in the beam may obscure at the gravitational deflection. An additional problem is the earth's magnetic

90

field. Electrons of even a few volts energy will feel a force due to the earth's field a thousand billion times larger than the gravitational deflection. This last problem is avoided in a static measurement of the ratio such as a weighing of ionized matter. However, this last method has the additional difficulty of requiring a high proportion of ionized to unionized matter in the sample being weighed. Of course all these problems can be resolved to some extent but it is questionable if an experiment of either of the above types can be designed in which all the adverse effects can simultaneously be sufficiently minimized. Probably a completely new type of experiment will have to be devised to measure the weight to mass ratio of the proton or electron. Such a measurement may detect a deviation from the law of constant weight to mass ratio. If such an anomaly can be shown to exist, there is the possibility of finding a material which would be acted upon in an unusual manner in a gravitational field.

Martin L. Perl[*]

---

[*]Editor's Note: Martin L. Perl is the recipient of the 1995 Nobel Prize in physics.

NEGATIVE MASS AS A GRAVITATIONAL SOURCE OF ENERGY IN THE QUASI-STELLAR RADIO SOURCES

Banesh Hoffman

Queens College of the City
University of New York
Flushing, N.Y. 11367

Essay Awarded the First Prize
by
Gravity Research Foundation
1964

ABSTRACT

Based on the asymmetry of gravitational radiation with respect to positive and negative mass, a physical process is proposed whereby negative mass could be generated inside certain celestial objects. This process could then account for the prodigious amounts of energy radiated by the recently discovered quasi-stellar radio sources,[*] it could provide an alternative to the synchrotron theory of the continuous spectrum of their emitted radiation. It could also account for the existence of cosmic ray showers of extremely high energy.

Negative mass may or may not exist. If it does, the according to both Newtonian mechanics and Einstein's general theory of relativity, it behaves in a most astonishing manner. For example, by the principle of equivalence the ratio of gravitational to inertial mass must be positive for all mass. Therefore, as is well known, positive mass attracts negative as well as positive mass, while negative mass repels both types of mass. Consequently, if a mass is placed near a mass -m, the two move in the same direction with ever-increasing speed, the negative mass chasing the positive. At first this seems to contradict the law of conservation of energy. But the particle of negative mass acquires <u>negative</u> energy as its speed increases, and the total energy of the two particles remains constant.

So disconcerting is the behavior of negative mass that when Dirac discovered the negative-mass solutions of his relativistic equations of the electron he was dismayed. But by imagining almost all of the negative energy states filled, he was able to treat the occasional vacancies as particles of <u>positive</u> mass and positive charge, thus arriving at the concept of anti-matter. Anti-matter is now treated as having positive mass in its own right rather than as being an absence of negative mass.

We propose here to take the idea of negative mass seriously, a major reason for doing so being the desperate theoretical situation into which physics has been thrust by the anomalous behavior of the recently-discovered quasi-stellar radio sources.[1] The idea of negative

---

[*] Now called "quasars" — Editor

mass is extremely natural in the general theory of relativity. Indeed, one can exclude negative mass from Einstein's theory only by an ad hoc assumption extraneous to the theory.

According to Einstein's theory, gravitational waves are theoretically possible. It may well be that they are not generated by bodies in free fall; but if they exist they should be generated when matter is strongly influenced by non-gravitational forces. In the special cases that have been studied[2], these waves carry away energy and cause a corresponding diminution in the mass of the radiating body. But there is a peculiar asymmetry about the energy transported by the gravitational waves: the energy is positive whether the mass of the source is positive or negative. Since this apparently arises from the Minkowskian signature of space-time it would seem to be of a fundamental nature. It has significant consequences. For unlike electromagnetic waves, which do not transport charge though their source is charge, gravitational waves are produced by mass and transport mass (in the form of energy). So if a body of mass m gives off gravitational waves of energy $c^2 \Delta m$, its mass is reduced to m- Δm, but if the mass of the emitter is -m it becomes -(m+ Δm), which is a greater amount of negative mass than before.

Let us assume that there is a quantum law, analogous to the law of conservation of baryon number, that prevents particles of positive rest mass from decaying into particles of negative rest mass. And let us assume that under extreme and unusual conditions such as might occur inside the quasi-stellar radio sources, and only under such conditions, the law is violated, so that "forbidden" transitions can occur, these transitions being linked to the weakest known interaction, gravitation, and requiring the emission of gravitational quanta of positive energy.

Consider what might happen near the center of an extremely hot and massive celestial object. The high pressure and temperature will subject particles there to intense nuclear forces which, being nongravitational, could cause strong emission of gravitational radiation. Particles of positive rest mass emitting gravitational quanta of sufficient size will turn into particles of negative rest mass; and further emission by these particles will only increase the amount of their negative rest mass. Some of the gravitational radiation may be reabsorbed by matter of negative rest mass, but much of it will escape

94

to the less central regions of the celestial object where conditions do not favor such transitions, and there it will undergo "Compton" collisions, giving up energy that will ultimately be converted to electromagnetic and other radiation.

Since negative masses react perversely to all except gravitational forces, they will be <u>less</u> buoyant than positive masses. (I am indebted to Dr. Ivor Robinson for this remark.) But negative mass is self-repelling. So, as it accumulates centrally, it will tend to cause instability, and part of it may ultimately escape from the quasi-stellar objects in eruptions that could be the cause of the characteristic jets associated with some of these objects.

It is precisely because the quasi-stellar object emits amounts of energy so prodigious as to defy conventional explanation that the concept of negative mass deserves to be taken seriously. For when negative mass is reduced within such objects positive energy is made available, and the greater the amount of negative mass created, the greater amount of positive energy released. Nor need positive mass always be used up when such energy is released; for if a particle of negative mass is sufficiently accelerated it can radiate further gravitational quanta, thus sending out more positive energy while falling to a yet lower negative energy state. (Since the inertia increases, the process need not diverge.) The violet shift caused by the negative mass will be negligible compared with the Hubble shift. Moreover, should any negative mass escape, whether in a jet or less spectacularly, the quasi-stellar object will merely be left with greater positive energy than before. Thus the mechanism outlined here could well account for the extraordinary flux of energy from these objects.

The electromagnetic radiation ultimately generated in the charged outer layers by the gravitational radiation would have a wide range of frequencies, and this could account for the remark-able intensity observed in the radio region. (The observed polarization is small, and it neither rules out the proposed mechanism nor confirms that synchrotron radiation is a major component.)

What happens to particles of negative mass that escape? They are unlikely to be present in interstellar space insufficient amounts to affect significantly our estimates of the average density of the universe. Since they repel all matter, they cannot form negative-mass stars. If

95

the universe is such that negative-mass particles can, on balance, "escape to infinity" there will be an effect of continual creation of positive energy in the observed region.

Since negative mass is not antimatter, a charged particle of rest mass -m meeting a particle of rest mass +m and the same (not opposite) charge could form with it a stable, loosely bound system whose mass would be merely that of the electromagnetic binding energy. Such an entity would acquire enormous speeds in extended intergalactic fields too weak to dissociate it. If it dissociated due to collision near the earth the +m component could cause a cosmic ray shower of enormous energy. The energy of some observed showers is puzzlingly high.

If a charged particle of negative mass were detected in, say, a cloud chamber and mistakenly interpreted as a particle of opposite charge and positive mass, there would be seeming discrepancies in such things as the energy and charge balances of reactions that might occur. It would be interesting to see if corroborative evidence for the existence of particles of negative mass could be found by the cosmic ray experimenters, for such a discovery would have momentous importance.

REFERENCES

1.   Proceedings of the International Symposium on Gravitational Collapse, Dallas (to appear).

2.   For an account of the work of Bondi, Brill, Weber, and   Wheeler, on this point see D.R. Brill, Annals of Physics 7 (1959) p. 466. See also H. Bondi et al, Proc. Roy. Soc. 269A (1962) p. 21.

APPENDIX
to this book

A collection of electrogravitics patents' cover sheets and relevant articles

Note: complete patents may be ordered for $3 each from:
U. S. Patent Office
Box 9
Washington, DC 20231

Complete patents may also be viewed at
www.google.com/patents

Thomas Townsend Brown

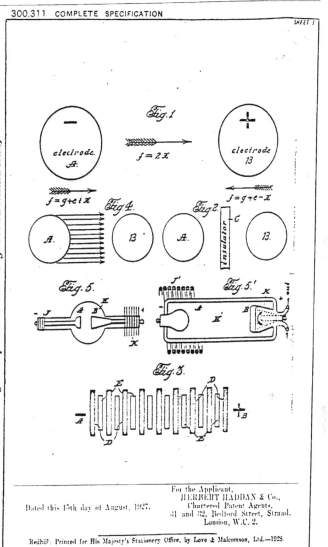

For the Applicant,
HERBERT HADDAN & Co.,
Chartered Patent Agents,
31 and 32, Bedford Street, Strand,
London, W.C. 2.

Dated this 15th day of August, 1927.

Redhill: Printed for His Majesty's Stationery Office, by Love & Malcomson, Ltd.—1928.

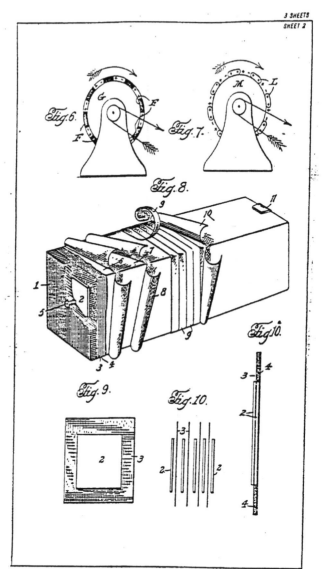

Fig. 6.

Fig. 7.

Fig. 8.

Fig. 9.

Fig. 10.

99

3 SHEETS
SHEET 3

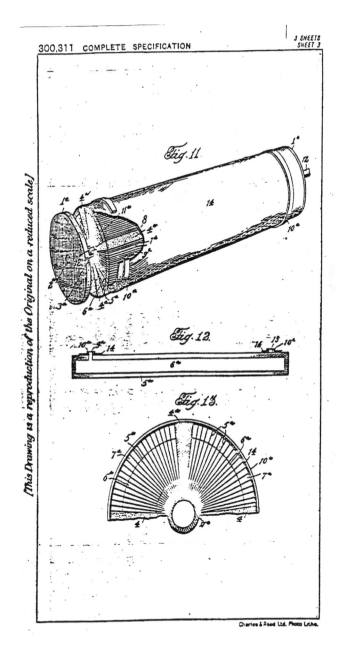

[This Drawing is a reproduction of the Original on a reduced scale.]

Fig. 11.

Fig. 12.

Fig. 13.

100

with the same idea incorporated in a rotary motor.

Figures 12 and 13 are detail views thereof.

5 The general showing in Figure 1 will make clear how my method for controlling or influencing the gravitational field or the energy of gravitation, or for producing linear force or motion, is utilized by 10 any machine or apparatus having the characteristics now to be pointed out.

Such a machine has two major parts A and B. These parts may be composed of any material capable of being charged 15 electrically. Mass A and mass B may be termed electrodes A and B respectively. Electrode A is charged negatively with respect to electrode B, or what is substantially the same, electrode B is charged 20 positively with respect to electrode A, or what is usually the case, electrode A has an excess of electrons while electrode B has an excess of protons.

While charged in this manner the total 25 force of A toward B is the sum of force g (due to the normal gravitational field) and force e (due to the imposed electrical field) and force x, (due to the resultant of the unbalanced gravitational forces 30 caused by the electro-negative charge or by the presence of an excess of electrons on electrode A and by the electro-positive charge or by the presence of an excess of protons on electrode B).

35 Likewise the total force of B toward A is the sum of force g (due to the normal gravitational field), and force e (due to the imposed electrical field), minus force x (due to the resultant of unbalanced 40 gravitational forces caused by the electro-negative charge or by the presence of an excess of electrons on electrode A and by the electro-positive charge or by the presence of an excess of protons on electrode 45 B).

By the cancellation of similar and opposing forces and by the addition of similar and allied forces the two electrodes taken collectively possess a force $2g$ in the 50 direction of B. This force $2e$ shared by both electrodes exists as a tendency of these electrodes to move or accelerate in the direction of the force, that is, A toward B and B away from A. More-55 over any machine or apparatus possessing electrodes A and B will exhibit such a lateral acceleration or motion if free to move. Such a motion is believed to be due to the direct control and influence 60 of the energy of gravitation by the electrical energy which exists in the unlike electrical charges present on the affected electrodes. This motion seems to possess no equal or opposite motion that is de-65 tectable by the present day mechanics.

It is to be understood that in explaining the theory underlying my invention I am imparting my best understanding of that theory, derived from practical 70 demonstration by the use of appropriate apparatus made in keeping with the teachings of the present Specification. The practice of the method, and apparatus aiding in the performance of the method, 75 have been successful as herein disclosed, and the breadth of my invention and discovery is such as to embrace any corrected or more refined theory that may be found to underlie the phenomena which I be-80 lieve myself to be the first to discover and put to practical service.

In this Specification I have used terms as "gravitator cells" and "gravitator cellular body" which are words of my 85 own coining in making reference to the particular type of cell I employ in the present invention. Wherever the construction involves the use of a pair of electrodes, separated by an insulating 90 plate or member, such construction complies with the term gravitator cells; and when two or more gravitator cells are connected in series within a body, such will 95 fall within the meaning of gravitator cellular body.

In Figure 2 the electrodes A and B are shown as having placed between them an insulating plate or member C of suitable 100 material, such that the minimum number of electrons or ions may successfully penetrate it. This constitutes a cellular gravitator consisting of one gravitator cell.

A cellular gravitator, consisting of more 105 than one cell, will have the cell units connected in series. This type is illustrated in Figure 3, D being insulating members and E suitable conducting plates. It will be readily appreciated that many different 110 arrangements for cell units, each possessing distinct advantages, may be resorted to.

One arrangement, such as just referred to, is illustrated in Figure 6 of the drawings. Here the cells designated F are 115 grouped in spaced relation and placed evenly around the circumference of a wheel G. Each group of cells F possesses a linear acceleration and the wheel rotates as a result of the combined 120 forces. It will be understood that, the cells being spaced substantial distances apart, the separation of adjacent positive and negative elements of separate cells is greater than the separation of the positive 125 and negative elements of any cell, and the materials of which the cells are formed being the more readily affected by the phenomena underlying my invention than the mere space between adjacent cells, any 130

101

3

forces existing between positive and negative elements of adjacent cells can never become of sufficient magnitude to neutralize or balance the force created by the respective cells adjoining said spaces. The uses to which such a motor, wheel, or rotor may be put are practically limitless, as can be readily understood, without further description. The structure may suitable be called a gravitator motor of cellular type.

In keeping with the purpose of my invention an apparatus may employ the electrodes A and B within a vacuum tube. This aspect of the invention is shown in Figures 4 and 5. In Figure 4 the electrodes A and B are such as are adapted to be placed within a vacuum tube H (Fig. 5), the frame and mounting being well within the province of the skilled artisan. Electrons, ions, or thermions can migrate readily from A to B. The construction may be appropriately termed an electronic, ionic, or thermionic gravitator as the case may be.

In certain of the last named types of gravitator units, it is desirable or necessary to heat to incandescence the whole or a part of electrode A to obtain better emission of negative thermions or electrons or at least to be able to control that emission by variation in the temperature of said electrode A. Since such variations also influence the magnitude of the longitudinal force or acceleration exhibited by the tube, it proves to be a very convenient method of varying this effect and of electrically controlling the motion of the tube. The electrode A may be heated to incandescence in any convenient way as by the ordinary methods utilizing electrical resistance or electrical induction, an instance of the former being shown at J (Fig. 5) and an instance of the latter at J¹ (Fig. 5¹), the vacuum tube in Fig. 5¹ being designated H¹.

Moreover in certain types of the gravitator units, now being considered, it is advantageous or necessary also to conduct away from the anode or positive electrode B excessive heat that may be generated during the operation of tube H or H¹. Such cooling is effected externally by means of air or water cooled flanges that are in thermo connection with the anode, or it is effected internally by passing a stream of water, air, or other fluid through a hollow anode made especially for that purpose. Air cooled flanges are illustrated at K (Fig. 5) and a hollow anode for the reception of a cooling liquid or fluid (as air or water) is shown at K¹ (Fig. 5¹). These electronic, ionic, or thermionic gravitator units may be grouped in any form productive of a desired force action or motion. One such form is the arrangement illustrated in Figure 7 where the particular gravitator units in question are indicated at L, disposed around a wheel or rotary motor similarly to the arrangement of the gravitator motor of cellular type shown in Figure 6, the difference being that in Figure 7, the electronic, ionic, or thermionic gravitator units are utilized. This motor may appropriately be designated as a gravitator motor of the electronic, ionic, or thermionic type, respectively.

The gravitator motors of Figures 6 and 7 may be supplied with the necessary electrical energy for the operation and resultant motion thereof from sources outside and independent of the motor itself. In such instances they constitute external or independently excited motors. On the other hand the motors when capable of creating sufficient power to generate by any method whatsoever all the electrical energy required therein for the operation of said motors are distinguished by being internal or self-excited. Here, it will be understood that the energy created by the operation of the motor may at times be vastly in excess of the energy required to operate the motor. In some instances the ratio may be even as high as a million to one. Inasmuch as any suitable means for supplying the necessary electrical energy, and suitable conducting means for permitting the energy generated by the motor to exert the expected influence on the same may be readily supplied, it is now deemed necessary to illustrate details herein. In said self-excited motors the energy necessary to overcome the friction or other resistance in the physical structure of the apparatus, and even to accelerate the motors against such resistance, is believed to be derived solely from the gravitational field or the energy of gravitation. Furthermore, said acceleration in the self-excited gravitator motor can be harnessed mechanically so as to produce usable energy or power, said usable energy or power, as aforesaid, being derived from or transferred by the apparatus solely from the energy of gravitation.

The gravitator motors function as a result of the mutual and unidirectional forces exerted by their charged electrodes. The direction of these forces and the resultant motion thereby produced are usually toward the positive electrode. This movement is practically linear. It is this primary action with which I deal.

As has already been pointed out herein, there are two ways in which this primary action can accomplish mechanical work. First, by operating in a linear path as it

102

does naturally, or second, by operating in a curved path. Since the circle is the most easily applied of all the geometric figures, it follows that the rotary form is the important. While other forms may be built it has been considered necessary to explain and illustrate only the linear and rotary forms.

The linear form of cellular gravitator is illustrated in detail in Figures 8, 9 and 10. It is built up of a number of metallic plates alternated or staggered with sheets of insulating material (Fig. 3). Each pair of plates so separated by insulation act as one gravitator cell, and each plate exhibits the desired force laterally. The potential is applied on the end plates and the potential difference is divided equally among the cells. Each metallic plate in the system possesses a force usually toward the positively charged terminus, and the system as a whole moves or tends to move in that direction. It is a linear motor, and the line of its action is parallel to the line of its electrodes.

There are three general rules to follow in the construction of such motors. First, the insulating sheets should be as thin as possible and yet have a relatively high puncture voltage. It is advisable also to use paraffin-saturated insulators on account of their high specific resistance. Second, the potential difference between any two metallic plates should be as high as possible and yet be safely under the minimum puncture voltage of the insulator. Third, there should, in most cases, be as many plates as possible in order that the saturation voltage of the system might be raised well above the highest voltage limit upon which the motor is operated. Reference has previously been made to the fact that in the preferred embodiment of the invention herein disclosed the movement is towards the positive electrode. However, it will be clear that motion may be had in a reverse direction determined by what I have just termed "saturation voltage", by which is meant the efficiency peak or maximum of action for that particular type of motor; the theory, as I may describe it, being that as the voltage is increased the force or action increases to a maximum which represents the greatest action in a negative-to-positive direction. If the voltage were increased beyond that maximum the action would decrease to zero and thence to the positive-to-negative direction.

Referring more specifically to Figs. 8, 9, and 10, red fiber end plates 1 act as supports and end insulators, and the first metallic plate 2 (for example aluminium) is connected electrically, through the fiber end plate, with the terminal 5. The second insulating sheet 3 is composed, for example, of varnished cambric sometimes known as "empire cloth". The relative size and arrangement of the metallic plate and insulating sheets are best seen in Figures 9 and 10. A paraffin filler H is placed between adjacent insulating sheets and around the edges of the metallic plates (Fig. 10a) and 6 represents a thin paraffin coating over the whole motor proper. 7 and 8 indicate successive layers of "empire cloth" or similar material, and 9 is a binding tape therefor. A thin film of a substance such as black spirit varnish 10 protects and insulates the entire outer surface. A phosphor bronze safety gap element 11 is connected electrically with the terminal (not shown) opposite to the terminal 5. A safety gap element corresponding with the element 11 is electrically connected with the terminal 5, but it has not been shown, in order better to illustrate interior parts. The purpose of the safety gaps is to limit the voltage imposed on the motor to a predetermined maximum and to prevent puncture.

The rotary motor (Figs. 11, 12 and 13), comprises broadly speaking, an assembly of a plurality of linear motors, fastened to or bent around the circumference of a wheel. In that case the wheel limits the action of the linear motors to a circle, and the wheel rotates in the manner of a fireworks pin wheel. The illustrations I have given are typical. The forms of Figures 6 and 7 have been defined. In Figure 11, the insulating end disk 1a has an opening 2a therethrough for an extension of the shaft 12. The disk 1a is secured to a suitable insulating motor shell, by fiber bolts or screws in any convenient manner, there being another of these disks at the opposite end of the shell, in the same manner as the opposite end plates 1 in Figure 8. The cells are built upon an insulating tube 11a disposed about the shaft-space 3a. Thick insulating wedges 4a separate the four linear motors illustrated. These thick insulating wedges, so-called, are substantially greater in body than the aggregate insulating sheets of the units. In some instances, however, dependent upon materials employed for the charged elements and the insulating members, this need not necessarily be the case. In each motor of this circular series of motors, there are the alternate sheets of insulation 5a associated with the alternate metallic plates 6a; paraffin fillers 7a along the edges of the plates 6a and between the insulating sheets 5a being employed similarly to the use of paraffin in Figure 8.

The rotary motor is encircled by metallic (preferably copper) collector rings 10a, which are connected with the end metallic plates of the separate linear motors at 9a and 13 (Fig. 12), one of these connections 9 being shown in detail where the insulating tube is cut away at 8 (Fig. 11).

It is unnecessary herein to illustrate a housing or bearings because any insulated housing and good ball bearings, conveniently supplied, will complete the motor. The potential is applied to the safety gap mounted on the housing and thence is conducted to the collector rings of the motor by means of sliding brushes.

While I have in the foregoing Specification outlined, in connection with the broader aspects of my invention, certain forms and details, I desire it understood that specific details have been referred to for the purpose of imparting a full and clear understanding of the invention, and not for purposes of limitation, because it should be apparent that many changes in construction and arrangement, and many embodiments of the invention, other than those illustrated, are possible without departing from the spirit of the invention or the scope of the appended claims.

Having now particularly described and ascertained the nature of my said invention and in what manner the same is to be performed, I declare that what I claim is:—

1. A method of producing force or motion, which comprises the step of aggregating the predominating gravitational lateral or linear forces of positive and negative charges which are so co-operatively related as to eliminate or practically eliminate the effect of the similar and opposing forces which said charges exert.

2. A method of producing force or motion, in which a mechanical or structural part is associated with at least two electrodes or the like, of which the adjacent electrodes or the like have charges of differing characteristics, the resultant, predominating, uni-directional gravitational force of said electrodes or the like being utilized to produce linear force or motion of said part.

3. A method according to Claim 1 or 2, in which the predominating force of the charges or electrodes is due to the normal gravitational field and the imposed electrical field.

4. A method according to Claim 1, 2 or 3, in which the electrodes or other elements bearing the charges are mounted, preferably rigidly, on a body or support adapted to move or exert force in the general direction of alignment of the electrodes or other charge-bearing elements.

5. A machine or apparatus for producing force or motion, which includes at least two electrodes or like elements adapted to be differently charged, so relatively arranged that they produce a combined linear force or motion in the general direction of their alignment.

6. A machine according to Claim 5, in which the electrodes or like elements are mounted, preferably rigidly, on a mechanical or structural part, whereby the predominating uni-directional force obtained from the electrodes or the like is adapted to move said part or to oppose forces tending to move it counter to the direction in which it would be moved by the action of the electrodes or the like.

7. A machine according to Claim 5 or 6, in which the energy necessary for charging the electrodes or the like is obtained either from the electrodes themselves or from an independent source.

8. A machine according to Claim 5, 6 or 7, whose force action or motive power depends in part on the gravitational field or energy of gravitation which is controlled or influenced by the action of the electrodes or the like.

9. A machine according to any of Claims 5 to 8, in the form of a motor including a gravitator cell or a gravitator cellular body, substantially as described.

10. A machine according to Claim 9, in which the gravitator cellular body or an assembly of the gravitator cells is mounted on a wheel-like support, whereby rotation of the latter may be effected, said cells being of electronic, ionic or thermionic type.

11. A method of controlling or influencing the gravitational field or the energy of gravitation and for deriving energy or power therefrom comprising the use of at least two masses differently electrically charged, whereby the surrounding gravitational field is affected or distorted by the imposed electrical field surrounding said charged masses, resulting in a uni-directional force being exerted on the system of charged masses in the general direction of the alignment of the masses, which system when permitted to move in response to said force in the above mentioned direction derives and accumulates as the result of said movement usable energy or power from the energy of gravitation or the gravitational field which is so controlled, influenced, or distorted.

12. The method of and the machine or apparatus for producing force or motion, by electrically controlling or influencing the gravitational field or energy of gravitation, substantially as hereinbefore described with reference to the accompanying drawings.

Aug. 16, 1960 — T. T. BROWN — 2,949,550

ELECTROKINETIC APPARATUS

Filed July 3, 1957 — 2 Sheets-Sheet 1

FIG. 1

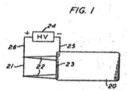

FIG. 2

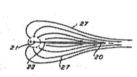

FIG. 3

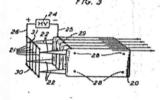

FIG. 4

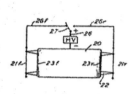

FIG. 5

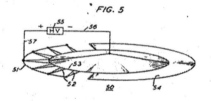

INVENTOR
THOMAS TOWNSEND BROWN
BY
Watson, Cole, Grindle & Watson
ATTORNEYS

FIG. 1

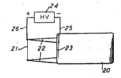

FIG. 2

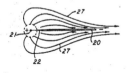

FIG. 3

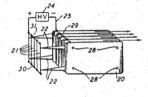

FIG. 4

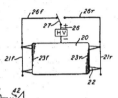

FIG. 5

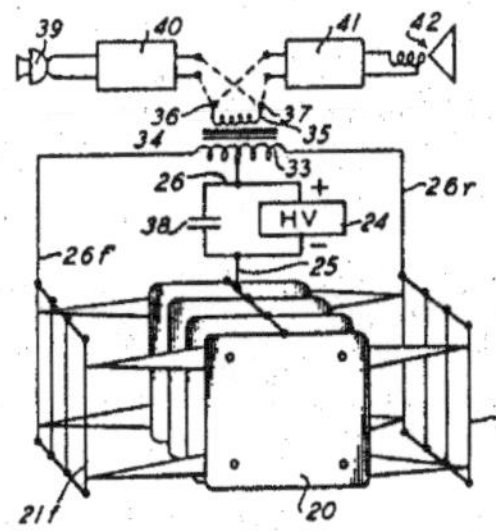

INVENTOR
THOMAS TOWNSEND BROWN
BY
Watson, Cole, Grindle & Watson
ATTORNEYS

106

FIG. 1

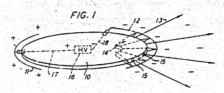

FIG. 2

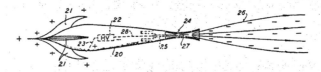

FIG. 3

AIR →

FUEL →

LOW VOLTAGE OUTPUT

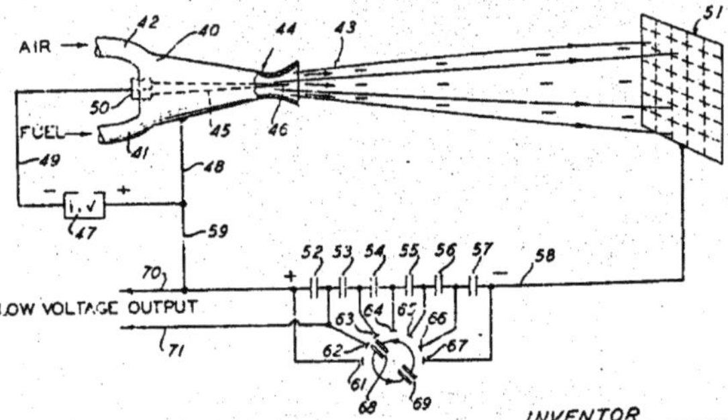

INVENTOR
THOMAS TOWNSEND BROWN
BY
Watson, Cole, Grindle & Watson
ATTORNEYS

107

June 1, 1965

T. T. BROWN

ELECTROKINETIC APPARATUS

3,187,206

Filed May 9, 1958

2 Sheets—Sheet 1

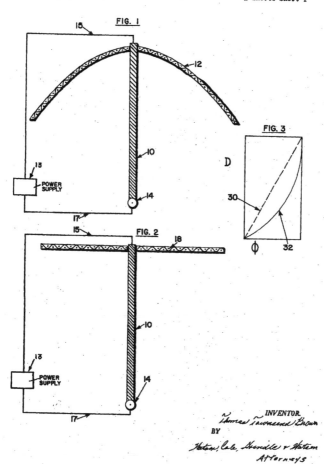

FIG. 1

FIG. 3

FIG. 2

INVENTOR.
Thomas Townsend Brown
BY
Watson, Cole, Grindle & Watson
Attorneys

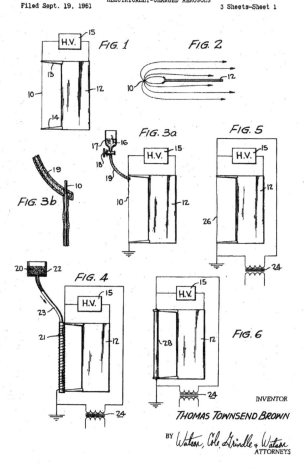

INVENTOR
THOMAS TOWNSEND BROWN
BY *Watson, Cole, Grindle & Watson*
ATTORNEYS

June 30, 1970   T. T. BROWN   **3,518,462**

FLUID FLOW CONTROL SYSTEM

Filed Aug. 21, 1967   2 Sheets—Sheet 1

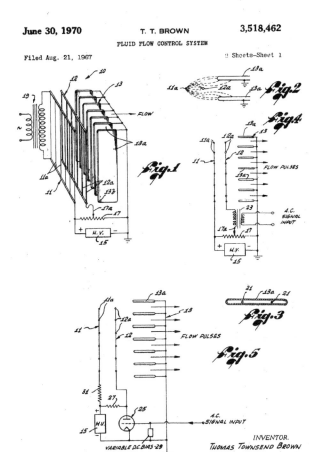

Fig.1

Fig.2

Fig.4

Fig.3

Fig.5

FLOW

FLOW PULSES

A.C. SIGNAL INPUT

H.V.

VARIABLE D.C. BIAS 29

INVENTOR.
THOMAS TOWNSEND BROWN

BY *Fulwider, Patton, Rieber,
Lee, and Utecht*
ATTORNEY

110

DATE-EVENT CHART FOR T.T. BROWN

1905	March 18, TT Brown born in Zanesville, Ohio.
1921	TTB discovers motion of the Coolidge X-ray tube caused by high voltage.
1922	Attended Cal-Tech; left school and joined the Navy.
1923	Attended Kenyon College, Ohio.
1924	Attended Dennison University, Gambier, Ohio where he met Prof. Biefeld (Ph.D., Zurich, Switzerland, 1900).
1926	Joined Swazey Observatory in Ohio, directed by Prof. Paul Alfred Biefeld.
1928	Maximum thrust measured on "Gravitor," 1% of total weight.
1929	Wrote article for *Science and Inventions*, "How I Control Gravitation."
1930	Left Swazey Observatory, signed on to Naval Research Lab, Washington, DC.
1932	U.S. Navy Department, staff physicist, International Gravity Expedition to West Indies.
1933	Staff physicist, Johnson-Smithsonian Deep Sea Expedition; joined Naval Reserve; soil engineer for Federal Emergency Relief Administration; joined FCC as an administrator.
1939	Lieutenant in Navy Reserve, moved to Maryland as a materials engineer for Glen L. Martin (Aircraft) Co., called into Navy Bureau of Ships as an officer in magnetic and acoustic mine research and development.
1940	May have joined the "Philadelphia Experiment."
1942	Lt. Commander, Commanding Officer of U.S. Navy Radar School at Norfolk, VA.
1943	Collapsed from exhaustion, retired from Navy, 6 months recuperation. Gravitor not recognized.
1944	Position with Lockheed-Vega, radar consultant.
1945	Went to Hawaii, continued research: (Presented ideas to Admiral Arthur W. Radford, Commander in Chief of U.S. Pacific Fleet, who later became Joint Chief of Staff/Eisenhower, 1953-57. No apparent interest was shown).
1952	Started Winterhaven Project in Cleveland, Ohio. Set up Townsend Brown Foundation office in Menlo Park, CA and demonstrated "flying saucer-"shaped disks electrically propelled around a "maypole."
1955-56	Presentations in England of his ideas.
1955-57	Leesburg, VA from Oct. 1955 to Feb. 1957; Umatillo, FL, Nov. 1957.
1956	Project work in France with his electrogravitation ideas for SNCASCO. Brown formed UFO study group, NICAP, in Washington, DC.
1957-60	Hired as consultant for Whitehall-Rand Project under auspices of Bahnson Labs (Agnew Bahnson) to do antigravity research and development.
1958	Brown formed Rand International, Ltd.
1958-67	Brown indicated he made no notes in his notebooks.
1959	Consultant with G.E. Space Center at King of Prussia, PA.
1960's	Physicist for Electro Kinetics at Bala Cynwyd, PA. Also semi-retired.
1967	T.T. Brown Notebook: October 23, 1967 in Santa Monica, CA.
1970	T.T. Brown Notebook: May 31, 1970 at Stanford University Hospital.
1973	T.T. Brown Notebook: indicates presence on Catalina Island, March 1973-Sep.1973.
1975	Honolulu, Hawaii working on "rock electricity."
1976-77	Sunnyvale, CA and University of Calif/Berkely: rock electricity work.
1979(?)	Consultant at Stanford Research Institute.
1980	University of North Carolina at Chapel Hill, Project Coordinator for XERXES Project.
1983	Project XERXES continued at California State University (Los Angeles); Brown residing at Avalon, California, as his health was more troublesome.
1985	Brown died at Avalon.

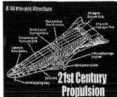

Electrogravitics

Research in the 1950's

Thomas Valone, MA, PE
Integrity Research Institute
1422 K Street NW, Ste 204 • Washington, DC 20005

21st Century Propulsion

Introduction

Electrogravitics, sometimes also called "gravitoelectrics", is the science of using high voltage electricity to provide propulsive force to aircraft or spacecraft of certain geometries. Its discovery is credited to Thomas Townsend Brown, a physicist who learned the secret from his professor, Dr. Paul Biefield. (There are indications that Biefield/ Brown experiments were predated in 1918 by Nipher's[1])

Unknown to many non-conventional propulsion experts, T.T. Brown's electrogravitics work after the war involved a classified multinational project. American companies such as Douglas, Glenn Martin, General Electric, Bell, and Sperry-Rand participated in the research effort. Britain, France, Sweden, Canada, and Germany also had concurrent projects from 1954 through 1956.

This article summarizes the recently declassified 1956 military document, "Electrogravitics Systems" by the Gravity Research Group of London (Special Weapons Study Unit)[2]. We will review the research highlights, the power range, electrogravitics theory, counterbary and baricentric control. This will show that Brown's discovery was a vital new addition to the aviation industry that became an integral part of the B-2 Stealth Bomber today—giving it an unlimited range.

Initial Studies

In 1929, T.T. Brown published his now famous article, "How I Con- trol Gravity", which outlined his experiments and principles of his electro-gravitation theory.

A curious fact revealed in this first article is the alignment of the *molecular gravitors*. These massive dielectrics provided the most propulsive force when the "differently charged elements" were aligned (with the voltage source). This sounds like crystal plane alignment and perhaps explains the article "Gravity Nullified: Quartz Crystals Charged by High Frequency Currents Lose Their Weight" which appeared in the same magazine but was rescinded by the editors shortly afterwards.

T.T. Brown's first patent, US Patent #1,974,483 issued in 1934, was entitled "Electrostatic Motor" and is a fascinating free energy machine as well as a propulsion source. Claiming an efficiency of a "million to one", Brown causes the massive dielectrics to be the workhorse of the motor, exceeding, in his words,

the well known pin wheel effect or reaction from a high voltage point discharge.

Much of what we know about T.T. Brown is from his numerous patents.

Though I was fortunate enough to correspond with him in 1981 when he was at the University of Florida. A sample of his detailed correspondence is contained in **Ether Technology** (which is a great introduction to Brown's work). An original drawing (shown below) of his shows the counterweighted saucer that optimized the charge distribution. The important detail is the power supply which went up to 250 kV, with a substantial force being displayed at 150 kV DC. Here we get an idea of the range of voltage necessary for successful electrogravitics.

Electrogravitics Systems

Only a few years ago, Dr. Paul LaViolette was in the Library of

---

Brown Comments on His Findings...

...In reviewing my letter of April 5th I notice, in the drawings which I attached, that I specified the power supply to be 50 KV. Actually, I should have indicated that it was 50 to 250 KV DC for the reason that the experiments were conducted throughout that entire range. The higher the voltage, the greater was the force observed. It appeared that, in these rough tests, that the increase in force was approximately linear with voltage. In vacuum the same test was carried on with a canopy electrode approximately 6" in diameter, with substantial force being displayed at 150 KV DC. I have a short strip of movie film showing this motion within the vacuum chamber as the potential is applied."

CREDIT: *Ether Technology* by Rho Sigma

CREDIT: *Ether Technology by Rho Sigma*

The first empirical experiments by Townsend Brown had the characteristic simplicity which has marked most other great scientific advancements, and concerned the behavior of a condenser when charged with electricity.

The startling revelation was that if placed in free suspension with the poles horizontal, the condenser, when charged, exhibited a forward thrust toward the positive pole! A reversal of polarity caused a reversal of the direction of thrust.

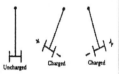

Further development of the implications of this phenomenon illustrated an "antigravity" effect. When balanced on a beam balance, and then charged, the condenser moves. If the positive pole is up, the condenser moves up (i.e., becomes "lighter"); if the positive pole is pointed down, it moves down [becomes "heavier"].

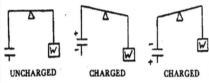

UNCHARGED   **CHARGED**   **CHARGED**

These two simple experiments demonstrate what is now known as the **Biefeld-Brown Effect**. To the best of our knowledge, it is the first method known of affecting a gravitational field by electrical means, and may contain the seeds of the control of gravity by Mankind.

The intensity of the effect is determined by five factors.

1. The separation of the plates of the condenser—closer plates, greater effect.
2. The higher the "K" factor, the greater the effect. ("K" is a measure of the ability of a material to store electric energy in the form of elastic stress.)
3. The greater the area of the condenser plates, the greater the effect.
4. The greater the voltage (potential) difference between the plates, the greater the effect.
5. The greater the mass of the material between the plates (dielectric), the greater the effect.

It is this last point which is inexplicable from the electromagnetic viewpoint, and which provides the connection with gravitation.

Use of Biefeld-Brown Effect can be used for electrogravitational steering of flying discs.

Congress in Washington, DC and looked up the work "electric" in the card catalog. Surprisingly, he found the listing for "Electrogravitics Systems"... a report that was missing from the stacks. When the librarian tried to locate any other copies, she commented, "It must be an exotic document" because she could find only one in the country which was at Wright-Patterson AFB.

Shortly after obtaining a copy, Paul and I agreed about the value of this report:

1) It validates T.T. Brown's experiments;
2) It lists the major corporations that were collaborating on electrogravitics;
3) The report expands the range of influence that Brown's research was having in the 1950's;
4) It includes the voltage and apparent power (KVA) requirements not real power (KW) for supersonic speed;
5) The report details the dielectric constant (k) goals for a Mach 3 fighter.
6) It shows the continuity from *Project Winterhaven* in 1952;
7) The report includes a list of electrostatic patents;
8) It had been *classified* by the Air Force for an undetermined amount of time which underscores its importance.

Prepared by the *Aviation Studies (International) Ltd., Gravity Research Group, Special Weapons Study Unit* in England in February of 1956, it defines electrogravitics as "a synthesis of electrostatic energy use for propulsion."

The report also asserts that:

electrogravitics had its birth after the War, when Townsend Brown sought to improve on the various proposals that then existed for electrostatic motors sufficiently to produce some visible manifestation of sustained motion.

As mentioned in the first section labeled "Discussion", both *Project*

Winterhaven (1952) and *Electrogravitics Systems* (1956) postulate "a saucer as the basis of a possible interceptor with Mach 3 capability." Furthermore, a dielectric constant of 30,000 is presented as sufficient for supersonic speed (barium titanium oxide has 6,000).

This section also discusses the creation of a local gravitational system by the craft which "would confer upon the fighter the sharp-edged changes of direction typical of motion in space." The ironic part of this comment is that there was no space program then so it is excusable that they would believe a vacuum conferred sharp-edged changes of direction. The concept of a "local gravitational field" will be referred to later in this article.

Later in the report, we read:
One of the difficulties in 1954 and 1955 was to get aviation to take electrogravitics seriously.

However, corporations such as Douglas, Sperry, Bell, GE, Hiller, Lear, and Convair are then described with an ongoing-project perspective. For example we read that,
General Electric is working on the use of electronic rigs to make adjustments to gravity.

Glenn Martin say gravity control could be achieved in six years....

Clarke Electronics state they have a rig, and add that in their view the source of gravity's force will be understood sooner than some people think.

This information makes the report exciting reading and gives it an air of suspense.

Equally as impressive is the listing of M.I.T., CalTech, Princeton, University of N. Carolina, and the unique Gravity Research Foundation as "all active in gravity." The report goes on to talk about a Swedish company, two Canadian companies and

a German company that have "woken up to the possibilities." In my view, the gem of the report is the admission:
Townsend Brown in electrogravitics is the equivalent of Frank Whittle in gas turbines.

Though we may not know who Frank Whittle is, the comment makes T.T. Brown legendary.

The end of the "Discussion" section centers on the thought that theoretical breakthroughs to discover the sources of gravity "will be made by the most advanced intellects using the most advanced research tools." The physics which these 1950's scientists thought would be required to produce a breakthrough in the understanding of gravity centered around nuclear research and particle accelerators. They emphasize the "urgency of the matter" and look to the country with "the biggest tools of this kind."

In the "Conclusions" section, they also mention that a new bevatron may be able to "demonstrate limited gravity control", not really understanding that it is a field effect which controls electrogravitics. The definitions of two useful terms are made:

Counterbary is the manipulation of gravitational force lines

Barycentric control is the adjustment to such manipulative capability to produce a stable type of motion suitable for transportation.

The conclusion that a Mach 3 fighter is possible with "megavolt energies and a k of over 10,000" is a valuable piece of data in this section.

Dielectric Constant and Electric Field

Before going on to the Appendix of the first report, it is important to discuss the meaning of "dielectric constant." Defined as "farads per meter", the dielectric constant, k, is the same as "capacitance per distance", which is the capacity to hold charge and avoiding discharge or dielectric breakdown.

Capacitors, or charge buckets, are rated in *capacitance* (C) and also by *voltage* (V) limitations. Picturing a capacitor as two parallel plates, the dielectric is placed in between them, giving it more charge at the same voltage.

The equation for a capacitor is:

$$C = {}^"k e_o A \cdot d$$

where

e_o is the permittivity of free space,
A is the area of the capacitor plate,
d is the distance between the plates.

This equation demonstrates that we can multiply the capacitor's ability to hold charge by its k value. Defining the dielectric constant of air as 1, we see that a k value of 10,000 would give a capacitor 10,000 times more charge in the same space limitations, which is important for aviation and for electrogravitics. The dielectric constant also gives the designer a direct control over what voltage he can use on the capacitor without experiencing electric discharges since,

$$Q = C V$$

where

Q is the amount of charge in coulombs

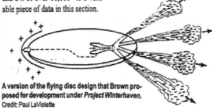

A version of the flying disc design that Brown proposed for development under *Project Winterhaven*.
Credit: Paul LaViolette

114

The point of mentioning this is that the charge in a capacitor is directly related to the electric field by an integral relationship. For a parallel plate capacitor, this becomes,

$$e_o kEA = Q$$

where

E is the electric field in volts per meter.

This leads to my primary reference which is the *Scientific American* article (Dec. '79) entitled "The Decay of the Vacuum" which describes the creation of matter and antimatter *without any input of energy* in the presence of an intense electric field. In what is called a *charged vacuum*, we should observe positron emission when an electron is accelerated through twice its rest mass, or about 1 Megavolt, in a short distance the size of an atom. The spontaneous creation of matter under such conditions is described by the authors as unstable empty space.

It is an intriguing fact that a supermassive nucleus, of atomic number Z=173 is sufficient to create this intense electric field and lower the total energy of the space. Creating a negative energy environment for the electron, the electric field would then be approximately $10^6 V/10^{-11}m$ (where $1010^{-11}m$ is the Bohr radius) or about 10^{17} volts per meter.

John Searl's Device

It is worth mentioning in this context the work of John R.R. Searl, formerly of England, where he constructed numerous craft purported to fly with high voltage. Throughout the sixties and the seventies, J.R.R. Searl produced many newsletters detailing the work he was doing. Since I corresponded with him in 1981, I also received some of these reports.

The importance of his experiments lies in the phenomena associated with them. In the 6/1/68 issue of the *Searl National Space Research Consortium* newsletter, Barrett reports that the ionization of the air and permanent electric polarity of dielectrics were common along with the antigravity effects. In the 6/14/71 issue of the newsletter, Bernhard Vaegs reports that "a pink halo surrounded the craft" and "potentials on the order of 10^{13} to 10^{14} volts" were generated. This is consistently found throughout the reports and was measured by the length of discharge and the standard breakdown of air (10,000 V/m).

Barrett describes in the 6/1/68 issue the *electrets* that are used in the craft as well as a vacuum layer that surrounds the craft preventing ionization breakdown of the air. (*Electrets* are materials that hold an electric field similar to the way magnets manifest magnetism). Notice how close Searl gets to the 10^{17} V/m instability threshold of the vacuum.

The similarities between Searl's high voltage propulsion and T.T. Brown's high voltage propulsion are so striking—just the voltage generation

John R.R.Searl in England claims to have developed an anti-gravity device in 1949. Searl was employed by the Midlands Electricity Board as an electronic and electrical fitter.

The principle of it is allegedly that, when a metal annulus is rotated at sufficient speed, the conduction electrons are displaced outwards by centrifugal force, so producing a very intense negative charge on the outside perimeter and a positive charge on the inside.

method is different. Searl uses an unbalanced high voltage charge distribution to direct his crafts just as Brown does. We must conclude that the Searl propulsion method is *electrogravitic* in the same sense as T.T. Brown's method.

The Gravitics Situation

This is another major report that is included in the *Electrogravitics* anthology[2] was released by Gravity Rand Ltd. (div. of Aviation Studies) in December, 1956. It starts out with a quote from Einstein looking for a precise mechanism of gravity and gives an overview of new details such as the operation of Brown's saucers in a vacuum and management notes on the anti-gravity industry.

A fascinating glossary is included which defines such new terms as: *gravihermal, lofting, counterbary, baricentric control, negamass, magnetogravitics,* etc.

A two-page journal reference list accompanies the report, with a summary of T. Townsend Brown's original patent specification.

Electrogravitics Voltage Disclosure

In the Appendix of the report (*Electrogravitics Systems*) we find a curious disclosure: "how, with the Mach 3 weapon in mind, to handle 50,000 KVA within the envelope of a thin pancake of 35 feet in diameter...." Since it is repeated later in the Appendix as well, it is important to distinguish this from 50,000 KW which is *real power*.

For example, electric utility bills are calculated based on kilowatt-hours (KWH) which is resistive load usage. KVA, or kilo-volt-amperes, describes *apparent power*, which is only used when AC power is in the system, such as with the volt-ampere rating of motors[7]. (The third part of the power triangle is *reactive power* which is power due to

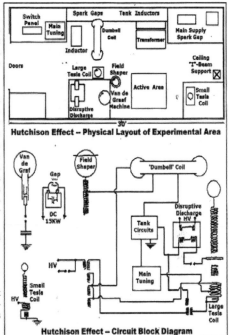

Hutchison Effect -- Physical Layout of Experimental Area

Hutchison Effect -- Circuit Block Diagram

capacitors or inductors only.)

It is known that Searl produces AC power but until the release of the *Electrogravitics Systems* the public was not informed that T.T. Brown had any AC component to his voltage supplies. This disclosure hints at the improvements which the aerospace industry may have been experimenting with to create a Mach 3 aircraft.

Along the same vein, Dr. Cravens, who gave Brown a high rating of "practicality", recently reported in his evaluation of T.T. Brown that older high voltage supplies always had some AC component to the regulated signal, which he wonders if it had any effect in the phenomena[8] This could be the most valuable part to this report, which is underscored in the following section.

The Hutchison Effect

In 1980, George Hathaway, a professional engineer licensed in Canada, formed a small company to develop and promote what is referred to as *the Hutchison Effect*. It is named after its inventor, John Hutchison, who liked to experiment with combinations of "Tesla coils and Van de Graaff generators" at the same time.

Much of the information about the "lift and disruption" effects has been reported at previous conferences[9]. Videotapes of much of the phenomena have been shown as well. Hathaway recently assembled a three-hour videotape which documents the TV interviews, reports, and actual events.

116

Electric Torsion Pendulum

Thanks to the *Ether Technology* text, Dr. Erwin Saxl's work was brought to the public's attention. In a relatively simple experiment, Dr. Saxl found that an electrically conductive, grounded torsion pendulum behaved strangely during a solar eclipse[10]. The period change was so dramatic that it could be timed to the eclipse precisely.

I had the opportunity to meet with Dr. Saxl's colleague, Mildred Allen from Mt. Holyoke College, a few years ago and obtained an unpublished paper of theirs at that time. The original experiments were performed with a fixed temperature varying less than 0.1C so the criticism that temperature variations could have induced the effects is unfounded.

Dr. Allais, who won a prize from the Gravity Research Foundation in 1959, also confirmed similar results using a conductive paraconical pendulum during a solar eclipse.[11] Alternatively, when the torsion pendulum was charged with high voltage, new phenomena began to emerge. An important relationship is the graph of *voltage* on the pendulum *versus its period*, which is found to be exponentially related. This is equivalent to a 5% change in inertial mass though the maximum variation in g is 10^{-5}.

The fact that gravity and electrostatic fields are related is not unusual, since various physical theories predict it. However, the nature of the interaction is just now being quantitatively analyzed instead of simple qualitative relations. Dr. Saxl notes:

When working as a post-doctoral student with Einstein, we discussed the possibility that there were interrelations between electricity, inertial mass and gravitation. These experi-

mental results make me wonder whether they may be so interpreted.[12]

The B-2 Stealth Bomber Connection

Thanks to Dr. Paul LaViolette reporting in his article, "The U.S. Antigravity Squadron"[13], there is *substantial evidence* that the electrogravitics research of the 1950's actually resulted in the B-2 Stealth Bomber auxiliary propulsion system.

Summarizing Dr. LaViolette's ar-

117

ticle, with references cited therein, we must emphasize the following table of important highlights. Together, they provide more than enough facts to make the B-2 a more fascinating aircraft than ever realized. Furthermore, the details which Dr. LaViolette uncovered below substantiate his physics theory of *Subquantum Kinetics* (the title of his book) which actually predicts that high voltage will have a propulsion effect when properly polarized.[14]

These exciting facts and more create a sense of excitement about the world's foremost aircraft. Dr. LaViolette argues that the electrogravitic drive will function better at higher speeds due to the shape of the craft causing better gravitic potential. Therefore, it is likely, he says, that the B-2 actually is a supersonic aircraft, especially since the leading-edge charging is primarily for supersonic softening of the shock wave besides electrogravitic capability.

House Representative Robert Walker was quoted in *Popular Science*[15] as promoting the idea of declassifying military secrets that will help commercial development. We hope that this trend will continue so the Spaceplane may also acquire an electrogravitic drive.

It is my belief, based upon T.T. Brown's research and Dr. LaViolette's theories, that an electrogravitic drive is a feasible propulsion method for the Mars journey. It is especially attractive since it uses so little power when it is operational. The complete reports:
• Electrogravitics Systems
• The Gravitics Situation"
• Negative Mass as an Energy Source
• The U.S. Antigravity Squadron
are available in the book, *Electrogravitics Systems: Reports on a New Propulsion Methodology.*

The 20th Century has been one of exploring and exploiting the interactions between electricity and magnetism. The 21st Century leads us in a new direction as we learn of the relationship between gravity and electricity. Our electrogravitic future is just beginning!_ *TV*

References

1) Nipher, *Electrical Experimenter*, March, 1918, p.743

2) Valone, T., ed., *Electro-gravitics Systems: Reports on a New Propulsion Methodology*, Integrity Research Institute, Washington, DC, 1994.

3) Brown, T.T., "How I Control Gravity", *Science and Invention*, 1929

4) *Science and Invention*, "Gravity Nullified", Sept. 1927, p. 398.

5) T.T. Brown U.S. Patents: #1,974,483, #2,949,550, #3,018,394, #3,022,430, #3,187,206 among others.

6) Rho Sigma, *Ether Technology*, 1977.

7) Boylestad, R.L., *Introductory Circuit Analysis*, Merrill Pub., 5th ed., 1987, p. 606. Also see "AC Formula Sheet" pub. by Integrity Res. Inst.

8) Cravens, T.L. "Electric Propulsion Study", AL-TR-89-040, #ADA 227121, Science Applic. Inter. Corp., Torrance, CA 90501

9) "The Hutchison Effect—A Lift and Disruption System", *Proceedings of the Third Inter. Symp. on Non-Conventional Energy Technology*, Hull, Quebec, 1988, pub. as *New Energy Technology*, by PACE, 100 Bronson, Ottawa, Ontario

10) Saxl & Allen, "1970 Solar Eclipse as 'Seen' by a Torsion Pendulum", *Physical Review D*, Vol. 3, No. 4, 1971, p.823. See also, "An Electrically Charged Torque Pendulum", *Nature*, July 11, 1964, p.136 by Dr. Erwin Saxl (lunar eclipse data).

11) Allais, M., "Should the Laws of Gravitation Be Reconsidered?", *Aero/Space Engineering*, Sep 1959, p.46 (Part 2 appears in Oct 1959, p.51)

12) Saxl and Allen, "Observations of Periodic Phenomena with a Massive Torsion Pendulum", unpublished manuscript, 1976

13) LaViolette, Paul, "The U.S. Antigravity Squadron", *Electrogravitics Systems*, Integrity Res. Inst., 1994, p.82, also published in the *Proceedings of 1993 New Energy Symposium*, Denver, Co

14) LaViolette, Paul, *Subquantum Kinetics*, Starburst Foundation; Brown, S., "Secrets of Groom Lake", *Popular Science*, p.54

TABLE OF B-2 BOMBER ELECTROGRAVITIC EVIDENCE

The B-2 Stealth Bomber is the "crown jewel" of the United States Air Force. The advanced technology incorporated into the design suggests that the B-2 may be our first step towards a true electrogravitic airship with supersonic capabilities.

Each of the B-2's leading edges is segmented into eight sections separated from one another by ten centimeter wide struts. Quite possibly, the struts electrically isolate the sections from one another so that they may be individually electrified. In this way, through proper control of the applied voltage, it would be possible to gravitically steer the craft. Brown had suggested a similar idea for steering his saucer craft.

The "crown jewel" of the US Air Force, the B-2 Stealth Bomber incorporates advanced electrogravitic principles!

The leading-edge sections positioned in front of the air scoops most likely are sparingly electrified so as to prevent positive ions from entering the engine ducts and neutralizing the negative ions being produced there. A summary of the advanced technology and its roots is as follows:

1) The B-2 charges the leading edges of its wing-like body, with high voltage;

2) The B-2 is shaped just like T.T. Brown suggested an electrogravitic craft should look, for maximum charge separation;

3) Northrup tested leading-edge charging in 1968;

4) T.T. Brown suggested that the craft should be powered by a flame-jet generator like the B-2 engine;

5) Aviation Week admits the existence of "dramatic, classified technologies" applicable to "aircraft control and propulsion" on the B-2;

6) Aviation Week also disclosed that the ceramic RAM on the B-2 outer skin is powdered depleted uranium, which just happens to have a dielectric constant of 3 times that of the high-K dielectrics tested in the 1950's (barium titanate oxide);

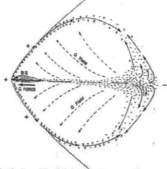

A side view of the B-2 showing the shape of its electrically charged Mach 2 supersonic shock and trailing exhaust stream. Solid arrows show the direction of ion flow; dashed arrows show the direction of the gravity gradient induced around the craft. Credit: Paul LaViolette

7) The B-2's Emergency Power Units (EPU) can work at high altitudes or even in space, driving an electrical generator;

8) Edward Aldridge, the Secretary of the Air Force, admits that the B-2 creates no vapor trail at high altitudes.

9) The decomposed gases from the EPU's can function as the ion-carrying medium, according to T.T. Brown.

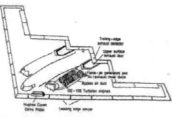

A view of the B-2 with a cutaway showing the arrangement of its flame-jet generators.

Flame generators were first suggested by T. T. Brown in the 1950s!!! Credit: Paul LaViolette

Ed. Note: See Paul LaViolette's book, *The Secrets of Antigravity*, Inner Traditions, 2008

119

THE ELECTROKINETIC WORKS OF
T.T. BROWN

by Steve Hall

INTRODUCTION

The purpose of this article is to present information on the little-known research efforts of T.T. Brown, particularly during the years 1957 through 1960. *Electric Spacecraft Journal* has reviewed a piecemeal video excerpted from a lab film of actual experiments performed by Brown, Agnew Bahnson, J. Frank King, and other associates of the Bahnson Labs in Winston-Salem, North Carolina.

Brown's main goal was to develop an antigravity propulsion system that would be spaceworthy. This lifelong focus led Brown across the United States and Europe in hopes of finding support and funding for his work.

Detailed information concerning Brown's research is difficult to find. If anyone has details from the Brown experiments, the *Electric Spacecraft Journal* would appreciate hearing from you.

HISTORICAL

T.T. Brown was born in 1905 to a prominent family in Zanesville, Ohio.

Sometime between 1913 and 1922 Brown obtained a Coolidge X-ray tube, with the thought that a key to space flight may be contained in this device.

His first experiments were set up to test for any type of forces that might be exerted by the x-rays to propel an object. He noticed that each time he turned on the tube it seemed to try to move on its own accord.

Brown explored this effect until he devised what he called a "gravitor." When connected to a 100 kv/dc power source, it lost 1% of its weight. He developed this instrument even before graduating from high school.

In 1922 Brown entered California Institute of Technology (Caltech) in Pasadena for one year, then transferred to Kenyon College in Gambier, Ohio. In 1924 he transferred again, to Denison University at Granville, Ohio, where he came under the guidance of Dr. Paul A. Biefeld, who was professor of physics and astronomy. (Dr. Biefeld was one of the eight classmates of Dr. Einstein in Switzerland.)

120

Brown and Dr. Biefeld experimented with charged capacitors and developed what is called the Biefeld-Brown Effect. This effect is observed when a high voltage capacitor is charged and exhibits a motion toward the positive plate or pole. Over the next four years Brown worked as a staff member at the Swazey Observatory with Dr. Biefeld. Also at this time he married and started his family.

In 1929 Brown wrote his first serious paper, "How I Control Gravitation," published in *Science and Invention*. Still, no one took his work seriously.

In 1930 he took a position with the Naval Research Lab (NRL) in Washington, DC. There he worked in areas of radiation, spectroscopy, and field physics. During this time he took part in the U.S. Navy's International Gravity Expedition. He also participated in the Johnson-Smithsonian Deep Sea Expedition.

By the year 1933, government funding cuts forced Brown to seek work elsewhere. He joined the Naval Reserve at this time and worked at any science-related jobs that became available.

In 1939 Brown and his family moved to Baltimore, Maryland, where he started working for the Glenn L. Martin Company (Martin Aerospace) as a materials engineer. This job was short-lived because the Navy called him to active duty. He became the officer in charge of magnetic and acoustic minesweeping research and development under the Bureau of Ships. It is speculated that at this time Brown became associated with the "Philadelphia Experiment."

Shortly after Pearl Harbor he was transferred to Norfolk as a lieutenant commander in charge of the Navy's Atlantic Fleet Radar School. Again it was reported that he was involved with the Philadelphia Experiment, working with

electromagnetic fields to achieve radar invisibility.

Tragedy came in December of 1943 when Brown suffered a nervous breakdown. After being sent home to convalesce, he was soon retired from the Navy, upon a naval physicians' review team recommendation.

By the spring of 1944 Brown was employed by the Lockheed-Vega Aircraft Corporation in California as a radar consultant. He then left Lockheed and moved to Hawaii, where he worked temporarily as a consultant at the Pearl Harbor Navy Yard.

During all this time Brown had continued to improve on his gravitor, and by 1951 had produced many working models. Brown had already envisioned the use of the Biefeld-Brown effect to propel air- and spacecraft and to act as a gravity field manipulator. The movement of ionized air molecules by high voltage fields was already known to produce propulsion. In fact, Brown had pointed this out in his patent #2949550. What he did not point out were his thoughts of direct gravity field interactions.

In 1952 Brown moved to Cleveland, Ohio and started his own project called "Winterhaven," which dealt with electrogravitics.

In 1953 he demonstrated the movement of disk-shaped electrokinetic transducers. They were two feet in diameter and reached a speed of 17 feet per second when a potential of 50 kv/dc was applied through a flexible lead, allowing the craft to circle a 20 foot-diameter path.

Brown continued developing better output craft, but due to a lack of interest in the U.S. he left for Europe in the hope of finding the support and funding needed to continue his research. In France he conducted research at the La Société Nationale de Construction Aéronautique Sud Ouest (SNCASO). Here he was able to increase the potentials to at least 200 kv/dc.

By 1956 Brown was again disappointed when the company SNCASO merged with Sud Est and funds were cut, forcing him to return to the U.S. Upon his return he founded the organization NICAP (National Investigative Committee for Aerial Phenomena) to study the Unidentified Flying Objects which seemed to him to exhibit many of the qualities of flight he was trying to attain.

By 1957 Brown was working as chief research and development consultant for the Whiteball-Rand Project for the Bahnson Company in Winston-Salem, North Carolina. The project was under the direction of Agnew Bahnson, president of the company. The project was set up to study antigravity. It is this period in Brown's life where the film mentioned earlier should shed some light on his experiments.

In 1959 Brown started working at the General Electric Space Center in King of Prussia, Pennsylvania. He worked there until at least June of 1960, according to the film footage. Brown also set up his own company called Rand International. The association between Bahnson and Brown is not known after 1960, but again tragedy struck when Agnew Bahnson was killed in a 1964 plane crash, and the project was suspended by the company.

Brown went into semi-retirement sometime in the 1960's and returned to Avalon, California to live.

As late as 1983 Brown was still involved in research efforts with a firm in Los Angeles. There he concentrated on a new form of radiation from space which was a carryover from his work with the Naval Research Lab in 1930. Cal State and the University of Hawaii were also involved. This new radiation held some promise in communications underwater as well as through large objects like a planet.

The life of Thomas Townsend Brown came to a close in October of 1985, at Avalon. A great deal of research information remains unknown.

T.T. BROWN'S PATENT

One of Brown's patents, #3,018,394, which was filed on July 3, 1952 and patented on January 23, 1962, says in part:

This invention [Electrokinetic Transducer] utilizes heretofore unknown electrokinetic phenomenon which I have discovered, namely that when pairs of electrodes of appropriate form are held in a certain fixed spacial relationship to each other and immersed in a dielectric medium and then oppositely charged to an appropriate degree, a force is produced tending to move the surrounding dielectric with respect to the pair of electrodes.

I have also discovered that if the dielectric medium is moved relative to the pairs of electrodes by an external mechanical force, a variation in the potential of the electrodes results which corresponds to the variation in the applied mechanical force.

Accordingly, it is an object of this invention to provide a method and apparatus for converting the energy of an electrical potential directly into a mechanical force suitable for causing relative motion between a structure and the surrounding medium.

It is another object of this invention to generate a varying electric potential by the motion of a surrounding dielectric medium with respect to a pair of electrodes supported in the medium.

The bottom electrode, in contrast to the top one, is many times smaller and appears to be all metallic in composition. It also has about 8 ribs which seem to be of the same material. They do not have any insulators attached nor can any plastic film be discerned around them.

As with most of the experiments observed in the video, there are flexible leads connected to one or both of the electrodes and sometimes an additional weight is also attached to the lead. Details about the power source are unknown. From what is known and observed, it appears that a very high voltage DC was the main power utilized.

This apparatus was shown at first to be hovering in place, bobbing slightly. Then, as if the voltage is increased, the object quickly moved up and the video moves to a calendar where someone circles the date February 28, 1959.

Photo #2 is a different type of experiment. The electrodes are similar in size and shape and are mounted to the floor. These open-ended, conic-shaped electrodes are used extensively, both in the atmosphere and in a vacuum chamber in other experiments.

Suspended by cords from the ceiling is a horizontal glass or plastic tube positioned to swing through the openings in the conic electrodes. Inside this tube are three squat cylinders which appear to be connected but do not extend outside the tubes. Whether these three objects are dielectrics, series-connected high voltage capacitors, or simple weights is not known.

High voltage power is applied to the conic electrodes and the tube swings back and forth. The motion is like a parallel pendulum in the high voltage field.

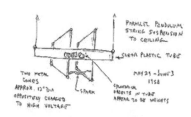

Photo #2

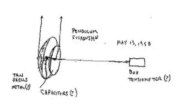

Photo #3

123

Brown may have been testing for variations in a pendulum swing that might show an interaction of the electric and gravity fields.

Photo #3 is included to show three squat cylinders mounted in series. These cylinders are in all likelihood high voltage capacitors between two dome-shaped electrodes. (Light-weight dome-shaped electrodes are used in many experiments, including those used in the vacuum chamber.) The whole apparatus is suspended from the ceiling with cords similar to those used in Photo #2. A horizontal cord is connected to what may be the negative electrode or a meter of some sort.

When power is applied, the suspended shells move toward the front or positive electrode. With this happening, it is possible to conclude that a self-propulsion device was successfully tested. It should be pointed out that Photo #1 also exhibits this effect. It should also be added that this apparatus could have been testing the pendulum variations as seen in Photo #2.

Photo #4 shows a disk that seems to be similar to some UFO objects. This could be deceiving though. The apparatus is shown only for a few seconds and does not exhibit any motion. It is simply lying on the table with the feet of a person shown in the background.

On top is mounted a small diameter glass or plastic disk. On the bottom is a larger disk of similar material. Sandwiched in between is a saucer-shaped metallic disk. This is similar to a flying saucer, but is, in fact, another electrode/dielectric configuration.

There are many unknown variables involved which make drawing any conclusions difficult at this time. Lab note data exists, but *Electric Spacecraft Journal* has not seen these to date. What tests were being conducted, and what results were expected are unknown, with the exception that T.T. Brown was determined to produce an electrokinetic transducer that could propel itself. If anyone has further information on the figures shown, other experiments or data, please contact us at the *Electric Spacecraft Journal*.

Photo #4

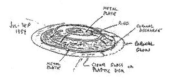

BIBLIOGRAPHY

The Philadelphia Experiment: Project Invisibility by William L. Moore and Charles Berlitz, Ballantine Books, New York, 1979.

Ether-Technology: A rational approach to gravity-control by Rho Sigma, CSA Printing and Bindery, Lakemont, Georgia 30552, 1977.

T. Townsend Brown Notebooks

Charles A. Yost

Charles Yost offers excerpts from the 1955 to 1977 lab notebooks of T.Townsend Brown (1905-1985).

Yost can be contacted at ESJ, 73 Sunlight Drive, Leicester, NC 28748.

Volume I–1955

October 1, p. 1 Leesburg, Virginia
Brown begins his first notebook, mentioning that all too often he has lost valuable information because he did not keep a notebook. These first notes relate to gravitation and electrodynamics.

October 7, pp. 3+
A note that Glen L. Martin and General Electric will be part of the space program. He mentions K. Jessup's "In the Case for the UFO" and refers to the ability of ancient peoples to move enormous stones. Brown mentions gravitational isotopes and suggests that in these early times (about 200,000 years ago), things may have simply been lighter in weight. [This is analogous to the idea expressed by Stan Deyo, that light used to travel much faster.]

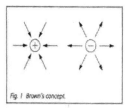

Fig. 1 Brown's concept.

p. 13
Brown's Concept (Fig. 1)
increased negativity (exogravitic field) causes:
    increase of gravitational mass (weight)
    decrease of inertial mass
    decrease of gravitational attraction
increased positivity (endogravitic field) causes:
    decrease of gravitational mass (weight)
    increase of inertial mass
    increase of gravitational attraction

December 25, p. 18
Brown suggests that gravitational potential is synonymous with the potential of the negative effluvium (Fig. 2).

1956

January 7, p. 21 Charles Brush experiments
Heat treating and working with metals causes metals to lose weight. Initial compression, hammering, etc., increases the specific gravity of metals, but continuing such action decreases the specific gravity of metals. Might also the tensile strength (for example, the ability of a piece of metal to withstand continuous flexing before it breaks) decrease at the same time? .

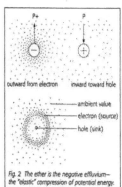

Fig. 2 The ether is the negative effluvium—the "elastic" compression of potential energy.

February 5, p. 37
Three factors affect the rate of fall (acceleration) of a freely falling body:

1. the intensity of the gravitational field
2. the susceptibility of the material being acted upon to the field
3. the inertial mass of the material.

p. 38
In a gravitational field,
acceleration $= m_g \, f_g / m_i$
f_g = gravity gradient force
m_g = gravitational (susceptibility) mass
m_i = inertial mass

Comparing m_g to m_i, or g to i,
$g/i = 1 \Rightarrow$ normal mass-weight equivalence
$g/i > 1 \Rightarrow$ heavy gravitational isotopes prevail
$g/i < 1 \Rightarrow$ lighter gravitational isotopes prevail

Brown suggests the use of a centrifuge (inertial acceleration) to determine if a "gravity" mass differs from an inertial mass.

April 7, p. 75
In a vacuum (10^{-6}mm Hg or less)—a simple vacuum capacitor will appear to flash as the voltage increases. Concurrent with the vacuum spark, an impulse force is notable in the direction from negative to positive.

p. 77
Successively higher voltages, starting at 30-40kV, and going up to 150kV, must be applied to allow flashing spark-over to continue. The anode takes on a reddish glow upon flashing and the cathode has bright starlike points. Impulse forces are on the order of thousands of dynes.

September 9, p. 83
Brown reiterates that grinding or pulverizing sand or rock into sand might cause it to lose weight. Friction or irradiation by sunlight while grinding are believed to supply the necessary energy.

1957

November 5
[Brown and Bahnson connect.]

Dec. 27, p. 98 Umatilla, FL
Brown discusses field shaping using shaped dielectrics (Fig. 3).

1958

January 1, p. 102 Winston Salem, NC
In the first notebook entry directly referring to the Bahnson experiments in Winston-Salem, NC,

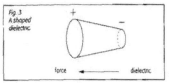

Fig. 3
A shaped dielectric

force ←————— dielectric

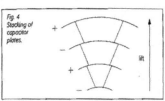

Fig. 4
Stacking of capacitor plates.

lift

Brown notes the stacking of capacitor plates for field shaping (Fig. 4).

January 5, pp. 103+
Brown describes possible details of the Adamski Venusian spaceship, reconstructing Adamski photographs and pointing out similarities to their (Bahnson/Brown) own models. The interpretation follows the lines of Brown's previous documents with thoughts of gravitic isotopes, aluminum silicates and rare earths in the field of a capacitor.

p. 108
Brown speculates on the cause of red coloration reported with "saucer" acceleration.

January 12, p. 111
Brown continues speculating on the "Venusian Scout Ship" design. The three balls are assumed not to rotate but rather to be used for setting flight direction and counteracting precession forces caused by a rotating toroidal coil (power coil).

January 19, p. 119
[Fig. 5.]

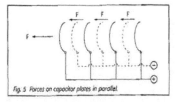

Fig. 5 Forces on capacitor plates in parallel.

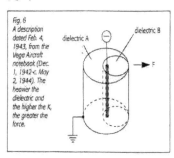

Fig. 6
A description dated Feb. 4, 1943, from the Vega Aircraft notebook (Dec. 1, 1942-c. May 2, 1944). The heavier the dielectric and the higher the K, the greater the force.

March 25, p. 124
J. Frank King reviews Brown's notes. Brown is still leaning toward the Adamski design. An RF inductor is introduced along with DC high voltage and a three-element electrode system.

April 7, p. 132 Walkertown, NC
[Fig. 7.]

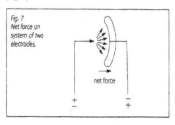

Fig. 7
Net force on system of two electrodes.

May 1, p. 148 Winston Salem, NC
The hydrostatic pressure developed by the oil within an insulating tube may be used to detect the force within a dielectric medium (Fig. 8).

Volume II—1967

October 23, pp. 21+ Santa Monica, CA
Brown notes, "During the period from October 1958 to October 1967 (nine years) no notes were made."

Brown writes about the construction of loudspeakers and air movement using high-voltage supplies. [The relationship with Agnew Bahnson, Jr. ends around 1965 with Bahnson's death. However, Brown continues to correspond with J. Frank King.]

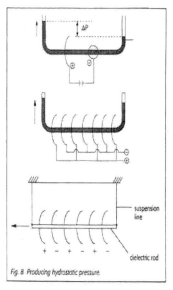

Fig. 8 Producing hydrostatic pressure.

1970

May 31, p. 25 Palo Alto, CA
Brown begins investigating the use of capacitors to detect gravitational waves. He starts with four 1µF, 25kV capacitors producing loud pops and whistles. Several circuit variations are sketched.

1973

March 26, p. 27 Catalina Island, CA
A triboelectric, high-voltage generator is described in which a barium titanate (high K) rod is rotated in oil (low K). The rubbing between the two is anticipated to make a high-voltage differential with the barium titanate (+).

March 30, p. 33
Red sand from Sorrento, FL undergoes tribo-excitation when shaken in a quart jar. Before shaking, the sand weighs 14 lbs. 14¹/₂ oz.; after shaking it weighs 14 lbs. 14¹/₄ oz. Brown is reviewing his idea that excited bodies lose weight. He considers that "sparking" to sand may produce a weight loss effect.

April 24, p. 40
Brown talks of Charles Francis Brush again and his work published in the *Physical Review* . . .

127

showing that different materials fall at different velocities. Brown is particularly fascinated with the rare earth elements and silicates (clay).

August 19, p. 62
Brown notes that Fernando Sanford measured cyclic, sidereal variations in the resistance of a wire, which could not be explained.

August 20, p. 68
Sanford observed a copper wire, 1mm dia. × 120cm long, from Feb. 17 to May 18, 1892. Its resistance variation (6×10^{-4} Ω) was cyclic under carefully controlled conditions.

September 4, p. 87
Relating to Sanford's book, *Terrestrial Electricity*, perhaps an electric field gradient surrounding the earth produces a sidereal factor of resistance change (apparent).

September 11, p. 113+
Many thoughts on the connection between gravity, capacitive storage, inductance storage and the variation of resistance with sidereal time. He considers that there is a gravity vector in the direction of electron flow. He realizes that a leakage current exists in the capacitor dielectric and that this may represent a direct conversion of electron flow to a gravity force vector. The gravity field of earth was therefore not being acted upon and the kinetic energy of the capacitor was not derived from the earth field. He relates that his early experiments showed the 'gravitator' force was a function of mass. Lead monoxide as a dielectric loaded in paraffin was usually used. The conductivity of the mass was never investigated (Fig. 9).

Both field and current are now considered as necessary to create a gravity vector within the semiconductive capacitor, requiring a very high voltage. The electron flow is from negative to positive, passing through the semiconductive mass and producing a gravity vector in that direction. Such a gravitator is considered a good sensor to detect variations of electrical and gravitational waves in the space around the earth.

September 16, p. 132
Watching his μA meter measuring currents through a resistance, Brown notes a sudden jump. The cause of such jumps is not easily explained, but is part of regular diurnal varia-

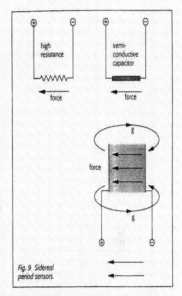

Fig. 9 Sidereal period sensors

tions. Brown settles into some long term serious measurements of voltage, resistance and current changes vs. time.

Volume III (missing)

Volume IV—1975

January 28, pp. 1+ Honolulu, Hawaii
Brown is in Hawaii measuring the output of his sensors (resistors, capacitors, etc.) and "rock" electrical variations. Certain rocks like granite appear polarized and do not need a diode in the test circuit (Fig. 10).

March 10, p. 36
A volcanic rock from Waikiki, 10cm in diameter, was washed and oven dried at 400°F. Copper print electrodes were painted on it after it cooled. The rock output about 60mV. When connected to the recorder it immediately showed regular pulsations about 1 second apart.

March 18, p. 42
Brown notes this is his 70th birthday.

March 24, pp. 43+
Rocks act like capacitors, they develop charge

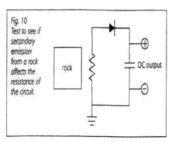

Fig. 10
Test to see if secondary emission from a rock affects the resistance of the circuit.

rock — DC output

and keep it. Brown speculates about the pyramids at Gizeh as being electrical generators or polarizers.

1976

April 23, p. 112 Univ. of CA Berkeley & Sunnyvale
He mentions making a sensor out of a tungsten carbide and carnauba wax mixture, keeping it under a high voltage field while the wax cools and hardens. A rock hard mixture of glycerine and litharge (PbO) also makes a good sensor.

May 6, pp. 113+
Brown mentions working with Jim Jardine of UC Berkeley.

May 10, p. 115
Brown finds high capacitance electrolyte capacitors to be good sensors of diurnal variations.

May 29, pp. 223+
Speculation continues on the great pyramids.

1977

February 10, p. 151
Brown's last entry, still recording rocks and capacitor data.

[Editor's Note: T. Townsend Brown died in 1985. ESJ 19 will provide some newly acquired data from Robert Dadd, who worked with Brown in the 1970s.]

Credit: *Electric Spacecraft Journal*, which is available by subscription from ESJ, 322 Sunlight Drive, Leicester, NC 28748
http://www.electricspacecraft.com/journal.htm

Asymmetrical capacitors
by Alexander V. Frolov

The electrogravitics was investigated by T.T.Brown in 1927 - 1965 but modern experimenting with asymmetrical electric capacitors become well known in 1990th as **"Lifter"** topic. What is the history of this research and what is most perspective direction of its development? I'll try to present my ideas on it

Some experiments were produced in my laboratory from 1994. The idea is to get asymmetry in the vectors of the field components. For example, in classical plane capacitor the plates are in attraction but the forces are contradicted. In T-shape capacitor two electrodes are placed in the same flat

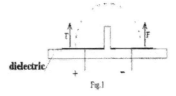

Fig.1

Electrodes are separated by "dielectric wall" to exclude electric discharge along minimal distance way between electrodes. The electric field structure is configured here to create co-directed electrostatic forces for both electrodes

Here is my article of 1994, published in USA and Canada http://www.faraday.ru/pot.htm
"To discover a solution for a non-zero unilateral resultant force, all we need is to note that the force line of the potential field is always perpendicular to the charged surface and take advantage of that fact."
Also comments by Thomas E. Bearden to this my paper are quite interesting.

Some experiments in Frolov's home laboratory, 1999

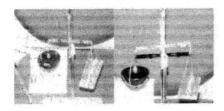

Small changes of weight of T-capacitor can be detected with simple balance scales. Voltage is 10 kV

Rotation test in my home laboratory. Look MPEG file here

Then the research group (Jean Louis Naudin) from France
also experimentally confirmed this principle (photos below). They named this asymmetrical capacitor as "Frolov's Hat"

In this version #3 by Jean Louis Naudin the wire and flat electrodes are two parts of the asymmetrical cap.

You can see video of this experiment here

The technology also presented by Transdimensional Technologies, USA

On July 6, 2001 http://www.tdimension.com/press_releases/press_release_6_25_01.html Photo from Transdimensional Technologies, USA

Some proposals for development of the technology

This technology is very complex for commercial application due to its high voltage equipment. You can try to calculate the size and voltage of the air asymmetrical capacitor of 1,000 kg weight (I made the calculations, they are not perspective). So, we need other solution

In 1995 I proposed the LIQUID DIELECTRIC version of the same asymmetrical capacitor. We produced simplest tests in Faraday Lab Ltd. Some weight changes were detected in **experiments of Sept. 2001** with asymmetrical capacitor (the jar and liquid oil dielectric).

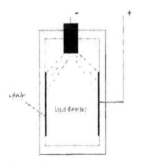

Fig.4

Force about 0,4 gram was detected. Voltage 10 KV was applied to the electrodes. Measurements were made with HL400EX digital scales.

Most perspective is research on **SOLID STATE GRADIENTAL DIELECTRIC.** The work is very complex for our small private laboratory since the problem is to get gradual changes of dielectrical permittivity in dielectrical material between two plates of flat capacitor. But we are sure in great commercial perspectives of this work and we continue the experimenting on the topic. The calculations seems to be very good http://www.faraday.ru/gradient.html

In 2002 Faraday Lab Ltd confirmed new way to get propulsion force by asymmetry of electric field without reactive mass flow, and this effect was detected when the power supply is off.

This data means that in this case the propulsion force does not require any power from external source. This effect named as "Active Force Effect". We are working on patent to apply the technology for aerospace and power engineering.

132

T. T. Brown
Experiment
Replicated

Larry Deavenport

Larry Deavenport is a hobbyist in electronics who attended the Texas State Tech Institute. He spent 20 years in maintenance at a copper refining plant.

The first time I recall hearing T. Townsend Brown's name was in a grade school science class during the early 1960s. At that time, NASA was in the process of developing ion and plasma rockets.

Like Nikola Tesla before him, Brown was a pioneer. At an early age, he was to make a remarkable discovery that would lead to the establishment of a field of research called electrogravitics.

While still a student at Denison University in Granville, Ohio, Brown noticed movement from wires of opposite polarity which would come in close proximity to one another. These wires had a tendency to attract while in the presence of very high voltage. Brown reported his observation to his physics professor, Paul Biefield, who encouraged him to do further experiments. The research that followed led to the Biefield-Brown effect and six U.S. patents for Brown.

In one of his experiments, Brown mounted condenser plates on a rotor. When voltage was applied, the rotor turned in a set direction. If the polarity of the voltage was reversed, the rotor would spin in the opposite direction.

The experiment which resulted in U.S. Patent #2,949,550, is perhaps Brown's most well-known. A large disk-shaped negative plate follows a positively charged wire (electrode) separated by a dielectric insulator. When two of these disks are suspended from a rotor mechanism and high voltage is applied, movement follows which is in the direction of the positive electrode, as illustrated in Figure 1.

The replication

During the summer of 1994, I decided to replicate Brown's rotor experiment. I machined two $2^5/8$-inch by $1/8$-inch thick aluminum disks, with a tapered edge.

Using a 16-inch by 2-inch wide piece of balsa wood, I built a crude, but workable, rotor to suspend the disks. Small pieces of #36 steel wire, separated by insulators, were attached to the rotor as condensers. A strip of $3/8$-inch copper was formed into a ring and glued to a $1^1/2$-inch by 18-inch tall PVC support for brush contact. The rotor was then suspended on top of the support with a glass door roller used for the bearing. The bearing was later replaced with a needle spindle because the original caused drag problems by creating too much surface area, which prevented the rotor from turning.

The power supply was a 0-15 volt input oscillator with a

Fig. 1 T.T. Brown's "electrokinetic apparatus." Figure 6 from U.S. Patent #2,949,550, granted Aug. 16, 1960.

To order any of the items mentioned in the article, contact Bob Ianinni at *Information Unlimited*, P.O. Box 716, Amherst, NH 03031-0716. Tel 603-673-4730.

The *IU* catalog is $1. The plan is part GRA1, and sells for $15. The kit is part GRA1K, and sells for $99.50. The 12V, 3amp power supply is part GRA10, and is made and priced to order.

133

25kV, 800 microamp output at 25kHz pulsed DC. The circuit diagram is illustrated in Figure 2.

When I applied the voltage, the disks behaved as if they wanted to turn, but they did not. I made several adjustments between the positive and negative electrodes of the disk, but still there was no rotation.

At the same time, I was experimenting with other power supplies. In one of these other trials, a 7000VAC, 5 milliamp transformer with six 10,000V capacitors and six 20,000V, 2 watt diodes were used. The six capacitors and six diodes were soldered together to form a Cockroft-Walton generator. This was set with spark gaps between them, and run in parallel with the original power supply. When the power supplies were turned on, the higher current transformer with the Cockroft-Walton DC ladder began to amplify the action of

the lesser powered 25kV, 25Hz pulsed DC supply. The aluminum disks began to resonate with every aluminum disk in the room. The disks behaved as if they wanted to move up and down, but the rotor did not turn.

It was several months before I tried any more experiments. Early this year, I was discussing the Brown experiment and the problems I was having with a friend. I showed him the rotor and mentioned the problem of having too much bearing surface drag from too large a bearing. We agreed that the bearing should be smaller, and decided to try a needle or small spindle. The changes were made, and on the first weekend in February, I started experimenting again. The new setup is shown in figures 3 and 4.

This time, the small rotor turned more freely; however, it needed to be balanced. Bearing surface drag and rotor balance will greatly affect the outcome of the experiment. Also very important is the size of the rotor bearing and how well the unit is balanced in conjunction with the size of the power supply.

The rotor began to turn slowly at first, at about 15 rpm. Several days later, I repeated some experiments with the rotor, and found that a ground connection was loose. When this was corrected, the rotor speed increased to about 35 rpm.

During this time, I contacted Dr. Paul LaViolette who suggested making the center of the disks more blunt instead of tapered. On my new 4-inch disks, shown in Figure 5, I took this into consideration.

One of the later experiments with the disks used a much larger power supply—0-50 volts DC, 0-15 amp input. The voltage was increased to

Fig. 2 Circuit diagram for rotor.

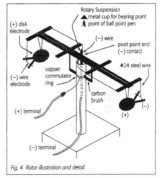

Fig. 3 The author's "maypole" rotor device.

Fig. 4 Rotor illustration and detail.

134

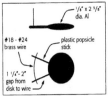

Fig. 4
Enlarged view of the disk electrode.

¹/₈″ x 2 ⁵/₈″ dia. Al

#18 - #24 brass wire

plastic popsicle stick

1 ¹/₄″- 2″ gap from disk to wire

various levels and special notice was taken as to what happened on the high voltage end. The original power supply or oscillator was rated for 6-15 volts with a 25 kHz DC pulsed output. It was originally purchased about 10 years ago for the Hagen device (U.S. Patent #3,120,363). In this experiment, a platform about 12 inches in diameter is negatively charged, while a smaller circular platform containing very small wires is positively charged. The slow moving mass of air and charged ions are supposed to generate lift. Regardless, this power supply worked well on Brown's experiment.

I also contacted Bob Ianinni, the owner of Information Unlimited and the manufacturer of this device. He first thought that due to the age of the power supply, a pulsed rippling effect might be generated from the capacitor. Since I do not own an oscilloscope, and have only a linear frequency counter built into my meter, there is no proof that this may have happened. However, after conducting tests using other capacitors (a 63 volt, 100,000 μF and a 63 volt, 15,000 μF) in place of the original 20 volt, 10,000 μF capacitor, I ruled out the rippling effect. If there had been a pulsed ripple produced from the capacitor, it would not have been present in a larger capacitor.

In the higher voltage experiments, the speed of the rotor increased significantly, from 35 rpm to about 60 rpm. This is after the power supply had reached 24 volts, according to the VOM reading. I checked with an analog meter for verification of input. This would have doubled the output of the high voltage to 50,000 volts and the current to about 1.5 milliamps. The rotor turned at a maximum speed of 60 rpm.

Several factors were responsible for the first breakdown between electrodes on the disks. High voltage power transistors had reached their maximum wattage, causing overheating, and the needle bearing on the rotor prevented the rotor from reaching high speeds.

Another experiment involved adding the Crockroft-Walton voltage ladder to the high voltage terminal of the power supply. This

stepped up the voltage, but dropped the microamp rating down. The rotor turned at about half the speed it normally turned, at 25kV. This indicates that voltage and current rise must remain proportional to maintain the effect.

An analysis of Brown's experiments

1 Voltage and amperage must be raised proportionally to maintain the electrogravitic effect.

2 As the voltage and current are raised, dielectric strength (K) or spacing between positive and negative electrodes must be increased.

3 Power or frequency of charging time must be increased proportionally as the size of the area is increased.

4 Changing the size of either electrode will affect the efficiency of ionic flow, if the dielectric and power source remain constant. The ratio in the size of the positive to the negative plate is directly proportional to the amount of voltage and current applied through a dielectric medium. With a smaller, high voltage low microamp power supply, the electrode on the positive side may have to be larger. On a higher voltage milliamps system, the positive electrode may need to be smaller.

5 Geometric configurations of shape may enhance or diminish the efficiency of the electromagnetic effect.

6 The electromagnetic effect increases in proportion to voltage, amperage, dielectric strength (the K factor) and area, when all of these increase together. It is lost when an arcover or breakdown occurs.

7 Some writers have, in the past, insinuated that electronic levitation is a product of very high frequencies and high voltages. Although a significant power increase may be present in this state, my experiments with the Biefield-Brown effect show that it is determined by the conditions thus described. Certainly, frequency, time lag and phase angle, along with all the formulas dealing with resonance would affect the efficiency of an AC system if it were used, but frequency and high voltage by themselves do not produce this effect.

In conclusion, I believe that the electrogravitic force is ever present, be it at one volt, one amp, one ohm, or 50,000 volts and 1 milliamp with a high dielectric strength. It is simply more noticeable at the high voltage electrostatic state, which is the opposite of the electromagnetic state.

Contact the author, Larry Deavenport, at 1823 Lawson Lane, Amarillo, TX 79106.

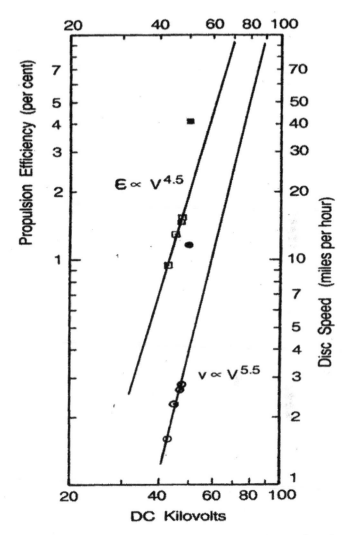

Disc speed v (□) and propulsion efficiency ε (o) as a function of average DC voltage V plotted logrithmically from ONR test data. Filled points are data from a separate test carried out by T. T. Brown. (credit: *Subquantum Kinetics*, Paul LaViolette, Starburst Foundation, p. 173)

The Antigravity Research of T. Townsend Brown

Many readers may recall the name of T. Townsend Brown (mentioned briefly in the previous article) as it was historically associated with UFOs. Brown was the first director of the now-defunct—but once very active—National Investigations Committee on Aerial Phenomena (NICAP), a Washington, D.C.-based lobby group that was very instrumental in the 1960s for getting congressional leaders interested in the UFO mystery. But what the majority may not realize was that Brown was also a very highly acclaimed physicist who held many patents and worked on a variety of highly classified projects.

It may well have been that Brown served as a very important "link" between the UFOlogical community and work being done in the 40s and 50s on what in scientific circles is best known as "Electrogravitics

Systems." There are even some who suggest that Brown's work in this field may have been assisted by his knowledge of the crash landing of a spaceship near Roswell, New Mexico. Because of his close dealings with the government and many private aerospace firms (both in the United States and aboard) he would have easily had access to knowledge considered to be on the "cutting edge."

According to Thomas Valone, a licensed professional engineer and head of the Integrity Research Institute (1377 K Street, N.W., Washington, D.C. 20005), some of Brown's early patterns showed designs that look very much like the familiar "flying saucer" seen throughout North America during this time period. In fact, in the group's recently published report titled *Electrogravitics Systems—Reports on a New

Propulsion Methodology*, Valone sees a very strong tie between Brown's discoveries and the development of the B-2 Stealth Bomber.

"There is," he says, "substantial evidence that the electrogravitics research of the 1950s actually resulted in the B-2 Stealth Bomber auxiliary propulsion system." In the report, an article by Dr. Paul VaViolette is summarized further reach these conclusions:

1. The B-2 charges the leading edges of its wing-like body, with high voltage;
2. The B-2 is shaped just like T.T. Brown suggested an electrogravitic craft should look, for maximum charge separation;
3. Northrup tested leading-edge charging in 1968;
4. T.T. Brown suggested that the craft should be powered by a flame-jet generator like the

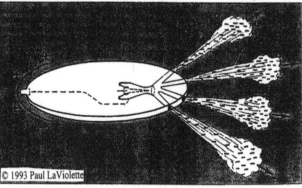

© 1993 Paul LaViolette

A version of the flying disc design that Brown proposed for development under Project Winterhaven.

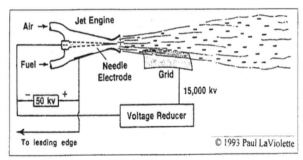

Air → Jet Engine

Fuel →

Needle Electrode Grid

15,000 kv

50 kv − +

Voltage Reducer

To leading edge

© 1993 Paul LaViolette

A high-voltage flame-jet generator.

B-2 engine.

5. *Aviation Week* admits the existence of "dramatic, classified technologies" applicable to "aircraft control and propulsion" on the B-2;

6. *Aviation Week* also disclosed that the ceramic RAM on the B-2 outer skin is powdered depleted uranium, which just happens to have a dielectric constant of three times that of the high-K dielectrics tested in the 1950s (barium titanate oxide);

7. The B-2's Emergency Power Units (EPU) can work at high altitudes or even in space, driving an electrical generator;

8. Edward Aldridge, the Secretary of the Air Force, admits that the B-2 creates no *vapor trail* at high altitudes.

9. The decomposed gases from

the EPU's an function as the ion-carrying medium, according to T.T. Brown.

From this point it is not hard to reach out even further and safely conclude that a great deal of what is going on inside Area 51 (Nevada's top secret military base) is based upon the work of Brown and others who long ago saw another way to reach the stars besides utilizing rockets that need very heavy fuel payloads.

After reading the available literature, even seasoned scientists have had to agree that Brown's propulsion methods may be our best bet in reaching out to the planets in our solar system that we might possibly be able to visit even now if these discoveries were not being kept under lock and key by those few ho would deem it necessary to utilize this valuable knowledge for their

own private gain.

John Searl's Work

British engineer John Searl claims to have built over 50 versions of his own "flying saucer," and has been receiving media attention—no matter how limited—for a number of years with his claims of having developed a noiseless, propulsion-free, levity disc that requires no fuel and flies vertically when taking off and landing. Searl even makes the bold claim that one of his craft actually flew around the world several times in the early 1970s...apparently without detection. It's claimed that "ultra-high voltage electro-static force fields are developed by segmented rings rotating in the disc's periphery. The craft's direction is controlled by varying voltage around the edge, thus producing unbelievable speed and agility."

The Searl Levity Disk...a man-made Flying Saucer goes aloft.

18

Et si le B-2 n'était pas seulement un avion ?

Selon des révélations dans les milieux de la recherche et de la construction aéronautique aux États-Unis,
le bombardier « furtif » de Northrop expérimenterait des techniques d'« électrogravité »

(Photo AFP)

Un avion est, par définition, un appareil de navigation aérienne plus lourd que l'air se déplaçant dans l'atmosphère en déployant sur ses lois de l'aérodynamique, alors le cas du B-2 américain, stratégique, semble l'aéronautique américain. Le dernier Salon du Bourget, est bien plus furtif, dans cette logique, à tendre, dans cette logique, à aucune famille officiellement connue, les moyens de transport aérien.

Pour mieux comprendre la nature des révélations qui filtrent actuellement sur les étranges particularités de cette machine volante, un détour par les coulisses de l'histoire s'impose.

Tardis que le B-2 était officiellement présenté au public le 22 novembre 1988, l'US Air Force déclarait que les technologies développées pour le mettre au point « allaient révolutionner l'industrie aéronautique américaine ». Cette phrase prophétique passa inaperçue.

BLACK PROGRAMS

Trois ans plus tard, William B. Scott, rédacteur en chef de l'hebdomadaire *Aviation Week & Space Technology* se pencha par un groupe d'ingénieurs sur un « programme noir » du Pentagone. Destiné à accélérer le processus de déclassification des technologies dont les chefs méritaient, à

leurs yeux, de bénéficier, ces « renégats » lui dévoilèrent quelques-uns

Thèse hardie

Alexandre Szames est un jeune journaliste scientifique dont les techniques d'échange font constituer le domaine public.

Personne ne fut choqué outre mesure par ces révélations. Et pourtant, ce qui semble être des grands secrets technologiques de la guerre de Northrop, dans le domaine public.

Le B-2 est bien plus furtif qu'il n'y paraît. En électrisant ses bords d'attaque et créant un potentiel et créant un potentiel plus « de plasma modelé sur la propre onde de choc. Ce phénomène se matérialise sous forme d'un halo lumineux

des plus noirs secrets de la charve-souris géante. Dont bénéficie son aile. B-2 présente se l'engin de charge aérodynamique actuelle sur ses bords d'attaque, un dispositif spécial lui permet de brouiller négativement les gaz brûlés en sortie de tuyère et sa cellule est également de un matériau qui, placé à la positive, permet d'absorber les ondes radar.

CANONS À IONS

Les moteurs du bombardier sont tout aussi exotiques. Conçus par General Electric (GE), ils servent effectivement à « pousser » l'appareil. Mais sa conception, son décollage et en descente, mais aussi la signature infra-rouge ? Cette explication n'est pas forcément seule valable. « Bien des aspects du processus de furtivité (du B-2) restant classifiés », indique l'US Air Force.

de couleur noir-orangée. Ses bénéfices sont immédiats. Le plasma agit comme un bouclier antiradar et permet au B-2 de voler à une bonne partie des ondes électromagnétiques et rend plus furtif l'atmosphère alentour. Le B-2 devrait une véritable savonnette volante.

En réalité, explique le Dr. Paul LaViolette dans trois études remarquables, cet étrange appareil exploite des procédés liés au B-2 est à l'ordre de « l'effet Biefeld-Brown, un phénomène découvert à l'aube des années 20 et défini comme la « tendance naturelle d'un condensateur chargé à haute tension à se déplacer dans la direction de son électrode positive ». On si l'on en croit les révélations d'*Aviation Week*, le B-2 est par nature un condensateur : ses bords d'attaque lui servent d'anode (électrode positive), tandis que l'aérodynamique (électrode négative) et sa cellule de l'effet Biefeld-Brown n'a reçu aucune publicité, c'est parce qu'il a constitué le contenu d'inavouables les modèles physiques couramment admis, ce phénomène est à l'origine d'une science « nouvelle », l'électrogravité (synonyme

ARCHIVES SECRETES

Si le B-2 ne constitue qu'un insigne aspect des percées technologiques accomplies pendant la guerre froide, un pan entier de l'histoire du XXᵉ siècle reste à découvrir. Peut-être des surprises-nous pas en révélant ici, quinze pages à chance publiques, comme le dévoile un Pentagone rendra 176 mitrons de pages de documents gardés secrets depuis plus de 25 ans !

Quant au B-2 se tiscturant appliqué à la prodigieuse scientifique, l'US Air Force prévoyait l'arrivée rapide d'avions-caméléons. Électriques, certes... mais totalement fail nu !

— Sous-titre et intertitres sont de la rédaction.

Alexandre SZAMES

Electrogravitics Systems:
Reports on a New Propulsion Methodology

THOMAS VALONE, ED.

REVIEWED BY LESLEE KULBA

The authors who contributed to *Electrogravitics Systems: Reports on a New Propulsion Methodology* assert that electrogravitics is not a dead-end field of research.

The 111-page book presents information indicating that antigravity has been and is being seriously investigated by leading aircraft industries as well as governments. An underlying theme is that T.T. Brown propulsion, once developed, will usher in an age of flight so revolutionary it will make all previous aviation, from the Wright brothers to space shuttles, constitute the Stone Age of flight.

This book can be appreciated by anyone who is interested in electrogravitics. It contains basic information for the neophyte (such as glossaries, patent lists and basics on T.T. Brown research), as well as clippings and information which make a case for the reality of electrogravitics technology.

Structurally, the book consists of four papers: "Electrogravitics Systems," from Aviation Studies, Ltd.; "The Gravitics Situation," from Gravity Rand Ltd., Div. of Aviation Studies, Ltd.; "Negative Mass As a Gravitational Source of Energy in the Quasi-Stellar Radio Sources," by Banesh Hoffman; and "The U.S. Antigravity Squadron," by

Paul LaViolette. All papers encourage serious research.

The book is thought-provoking. "What is gravity?" it asks; a question Newton and Einstein did not satisfactorily explain. Experts have told us: "It just is."

Electrogravitics Systems looks beyond, and asks how fast is gravity if not an instantaneous action-at-a-distance. Does it travel in waves? Does gravitational force, like other forces, generate heat? If so, how much?

The book makes some interesting points. For example, gravity may be the only force that is not quantized. It also states that all fundamental forces (e.g., electricity and magnetism) appear to exist in the form of opposites (poles). So, why shouldn't gravity have its opposite—negative gravity? Since gravitational force is dependent only on two or more masses and the absolute value of the distances separating them, the quest for antigravity then takes on the form of a quest for antimatter, not an uncommon task for modern physicists.

Questions are raised throughout the book, and solutions remain distant, though it is pointed out that the most satisfactory theo-

ries usually are simplistic in explanation and application.

Having made a theoretical case for electrogravitics, the book also makes a historical one. Hints of electrogravitics in the history of aviation, revealed through developments and statements made by major aircraft industries in articles from *Aviation Report* in the mid-1950s, are reprinted. T.T. Brown's work is described in detail.

With optimism, the book repeatedly states that the breakthroughs in antigravity devices are almost guaranteed to come from big industry which can pour grand sums of money into extensive research and development facilities.

The paper by Paul LaViolette was an intriguing speculation that the B-2 stealth bomber operated on T.T. Brown's principle of propulsion. Statements from government and ex-government workers and officials were shown to fit in nicely with this possibility. LaViolette argues that several disclosed as well as probable technological details of this classified design are consistent with design specifications for a would-be T.T. Brown aircraft.

Electrogravitics Systems was published by the Integrity Research Institute, 1377 K Street NW, Suite 204, Washington, D.C. 20005. It retails for $15.

140

----- Original Message -----
From: "Peter S Hunt" petershunt@email.msn.com
To: iri@erols.com
Sent: Thursday, April 25, 2002 3:23 PM
Subject: Electrogravitics

Dear Sir:

I was not fully surprised that the B-2 utilizes some non-combustive form of propulsion. When it first came out in the press I had some extended – in time – correspondence with the House Armed Services Committee on it's true stealth capacity. I pointed out that one of the dominant products of combustion was highly turbulent water vapor and that Raytheon was selling world wide radar systems tuned to this H_2O molecule which with Doppler analysis the signature of highly turbulent water vapor was easy to spot in the atmosphere (used for storm warnings). Hence any one searching for a B-2 powered with a jet engine would utilizing this weather radar would have a nice "V" indicating where the stealth bomber was as it flew across the sky.

Hardly stealth. The Committee made some inquiries as to the validity of my assertion and were fed some baloney about the heat shielding about the jet exhausts. When put to me I pointed out that the heat signature was not what I was talking about and without a nuclear transformation the water vapor would still identify the B-2.

The next inquiry brought some more smoke and mirrors and then I was just told to forget it. In line with this some alternative form of propulsion for the B-2 would make sense, at least while over unfriendly territory. I do believe, however, that it has jet engines for take off and perhaps cruise and is likely a hybrid in it's propulsion systems.

On a further issue do the TT Brown update machines (you have some video material on them from NASA) indicate any shielding in terms of mass in it's angular acceleration?

With every good wish,

Peter S. Hunt

141

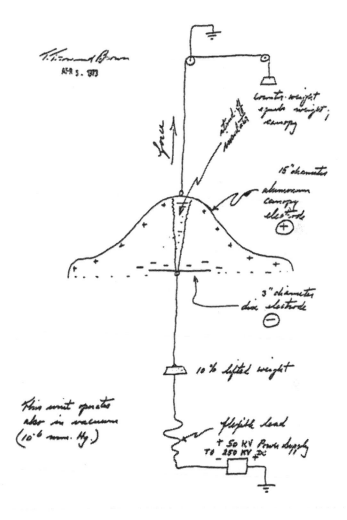

Original diagram from T. T. Brown stamped April 5, 1973 for a simple electrogravitics experiment. Brown states: **"This unit operates also in vacuum (10^{-6} mm Hg)".** (Sigma, Rho, *Ether-Technology, A rational approach to gravity-control*, CSA, 1977, p. 49)

The Townsend Brown Electro-Gravity Device. A comprehensive evaluation by the Office of Naval Research, with accompanying documents, issued **Sept. 15, 1952**. Every page was marked "confidential" until the classification of the report was cancelled by ONR. Detailed report with a surprise at the end. # 612 22 pg. $6

Thomas Townsend Brown: Bahnson Lab 1958-1960. This rare find, supplied by Sev Bonnie, a friend of the Bahnson family, is a documentary recorded originally in 8 mm film. Though silent, it is in color and reveals short segments of all of the Brown-Bahnson laboratory experiments. Specially designed craft levitate with electrogravitic propulsion (as described in Steve Hall's article in this book).   #606   approx. 1 hour DVD $20

SubQuantum Kinetics: The Alchemy of Creation. by Dr. Paul LaViolette. A masterpiece of theoretical work predicting electrogravitic forces and more. An entire chapter is devoted to electrogravitics. Topics include matter, fields, and forces based on systems science.
    #605   268 pg. book $25

Electrogravitics II. Thomas Valone PhD. Volume II of anthology that continues *Electrogravitics Systems* with original articles by T. T. Brown including, "How I Control Gravitation" and "Towards Flight without Stress or Strain...or Weight" as well as his complete project Winterhaven proposal; electrogravitics theory and experiment by Dr. T. Musha, physicist for Honda; biography of T.T. Brown. FREE narrated slide show CD upon request with purchase. #614 120 pg. book $15

Future Energy: Proceedings of the First International Conference on Future Energy. Papers from the 1999 three-day COFE symposium featuring more than 14 scientists, most with visual presentations of their breakthroughs in energy. Also includes invited papers. FREE audio CD-ROM with 20 hours of digital audio lectures of COFE speakers on request with purchase. #802   250 pg. book $40

143

ORDERING INFORMATION:
Shipping cost is $5 for U.S. residents. Add $7 for Canada. Add $15 for postage overseas. Send check, money order or charge card number to Integrity Research Institute, 5020 Sunnyside Avenue, Suite 209, Beltsville MD 20705. Call 888-802-5243 or 202-452-7674 for orders or publication catalog or visit **www.IntegrityResearchInstitute.org** to order online
Email: IRI@starpower.net

FOR MORE INFORMATION ON T.T. BROWN:

http://qualight.com/ - New biography

http://www.ttbrown.com/ - Historical website

http://peswiki.com/index.php/Directory:Thomas_Townsend_Brown

http://www.padrak.com/ine/INE7.html - T.T. Brown conference report

http://www.bitdig.com/torrent/other/download-1167419/Thomas-Townsend-Brown-Bahnson-Lab-1958-1960-zip.html - Brown-Bahnson Lab

End Note

If you would like to receive a FREE copy of Dr. Valone's "Progress in Future Energy" 30-minute DVD, send an email, fax or letter requesting "Free DVD" with your postal mailing address, anywhere in the world. You will also receive our latest catalog as well.

Made in United States
Troutdale, OR
10/29/2024

24227539R00082